BIKER'S HANDBOOK

Becoming Part of the MOTORCYCLE CULTURE

JAY BARBIERI

with foreword by Michele Smith

MOTORBOOKS

Acknowledgments

My Crew: Darryl, Ronnie, Mike, Mark, Albert, Bobby, Big Ray, Ray S., Fast Eddie, Scotty, Kevin, Johnny, Paul and Patrick. I have had the best times of my life riding with these guys, many of whom are included in this book.

The women in my life: My wife Suzanne. You'll never feel good on a bike if your girlfriend or spouse doesn't support you. Thank you for never asking me to stop riding and always encouraging my passion, you're the best sweetie. I love you.

Candy, thank you for helping me turn this book into a reality. See you next week. Same time, same place. Ruth Wald, when I started writing this book I actually broke spell check (yes, it's possible). Ruth you did an incredible job of deciphering what I was trying to say...Thank you!

Illustrations by Thunder. All photos, unless otherwise noted, by Jay Barbieri, Ron Caruso, Mike Dezaio, Darryl Sage, Mark Yonadi, and Albert Yonadi

First published in 2007 by MBI Motorbooks, an imprint of MBI Publishing Company LLC, Galtier Plaza, Suite 200, 380 Jackson Street, St. Paul, MN 55101 USA

Motorbooks titles are also available at discounts in bulk quantity for industrial or sales-promotional use. For details write to Special Sales Manager at MBI Publishing Company, Galtier Plaza, Suite 200, 380 Jackson Street, St. Paul, MN 55101 USA.

To find out more about our books, join us online at www.motorbooks.com.

Library of Congress Cataloging-in-Publication Data

Barbieri, Jay, 1964
  Biker's handbook : becoming part of the motorcycle culture / by Jay
Barbieri.
     p. cm.
  ISBN: 978-0-7603-3210-8 (softbound)
  1. Motorcycling–United States. 2. Motorcyclists–United States.
I.Title.
  GV1059.52.B37 2007
  796.7–dc22

                                    2007029400

Editor: Peter Schletty
Interior Designer: James Kegley
Cover Designer: Michael Cawcutt

Printed in China

CONTENTS

Dedications 7

Foreword 9

Introduction 10

Chapter One
Get It Straight: American Motorcycles 12

Chapter Two
How to Be a Cheap SOB Without Looking Like One 42

Chapter Three
Planning a Trip: This Time It Doesn't Mean Finding the Guy with the Best Dope 62

Chapter Four
Time to Get Going, But How? 74

Chapter Five
Don't Be "That Guy" . . . You Know Exactly What I Mean! 90

Chapter Six
Rally Time: Laconia, Daytona, and Sturgis 96

Chapter Seven
Any Excuse to Ride 160

Appendix 166

Index 172

STRAIGHT TALK

about *Biker's Handbook: Becoming Part of the Motorcycle Culture*

Just about everybody in the V-twin motorcycle aftermarket knows Jay Barbieri. Besides being a TV producer for *American Thunder* on SPEED Channel, Jay is genuinely into motorcycles. What you may not know is that Jay has a very quick wit and a great—though twisted—sense of humor. He puts his many years of riding experience and a good dollop of that sense of humor to work in *Biker's Handbook: Becoming Part of the Motorcycle Culture*. If you are new to the two-wheeled lifestyle, do what Jay tells you and you'll be fine. If you're already a biker, you'll laugh your butt off because Jay's accounts of the good, bad, and ugly experiences of living the lifestyle ring hilariously true.

Dave Nichols
Editor, *Easyriders* and *V-Twin* magazines

Having worked and partied with Jay for the last few years, I can attest to the fact that he's a crazy bastard. As for his book, I heartily recommend it. It's a great read, informative and entertaining. In his own free-wheeling way, Jay tells you what you need to know about bike events and the motorcycle subculture to fit right in and enjoy the ride. Definitely read it with a cold one at hand, in a place where you can laugh as loud as you want.

Chris Maida
Editor, *American Iron Magazine*

DEDICATIONS
I dedicate this book to two people:
My father, Edmund Barbieri, and my uncle John Kozej

My father was the reason I became obsessed with motorcycles. Although he fought me tooth and nail when it came to riding and wanting one, he did teach me how to ride, and he respected my passion. Before his untimely death in 2004, one of the last things he said to me was "I think this motorcycle thing might just work out for you."

My mother and father on their Harley-Davidson in the early 1960s.

I bought my first Harley from my uncle John Kozej. As a kid, I worked for him as a carpenter and the one thing he taught me that no education could provide was common sense. Common sense and the American motorcycle culture go hand in hand.

Thank you both for being strong guiding male role models for me in two very different ways.

My uncle on his early-1960s custom Triumph bobber.

FOREWORD

In 1997, I became the host of *American Thunder* on SPEED Channel. Since then, *American Thunder* has become the longest-running, number-one-rated motorcycle magazine show ever, and I have become immersed in the American motorcycle culture and am seen as an American motorcycle icon.

My duties as host of the show include traveling the country and interviewing custom bike builders and motorcycle enthusiasts as well as attending various motorcycle events and rallies, such as Sturgis Bike Week, Canada's International Supershow, Carlisle Bike Fest, Laughlin River Run, and Daytona Bike Week, to name a few.

In 2004, I met Jay Barbieri, who was brought on as a new producer of *American Thunder*. I wasn't quite sure what to expect, as I have seen several producers come and go over the years and not all of them have been knowledgeable about bikes. My first impression of Jay was "Oh no, this guy is just too Hollywood." I thought he was a little rock star–ish, and I was hoping that he wasn't one of those guys who trades in his loafers for motorcycle boots on the weekends. He really didn't strike me as a guy who knew a damn thing about motorcycles and the people who ride them. Boy, was I wrong!

Jay was not only familiar with the culture but practically a fixture in it. His knowledge of everything from building a bike to adapting to every riding situation instantly cemented our relationship. Since then we have become close friends and colleagues. It's always nice to work with someone who gets it!

For years I have fielded thousands of questions from new riders about the dos and don'ts in our world, and I've often wished I could give them the perfect answer or at least send them in the right direction. But now I can tell them everything they need to know is in *Biker's Handbook*.

Not only does this book offer factual and insightful information, but my pal Jay has some great stories here about being on the road and attending hundreds of rallies himself. Trust me when I say this: I have worked with him for several years now, and as unbelievable as it may seem, they are all true. It's these life experiences that make him a respected and credible authority in this unique subculture. In my opinion, *Biker's Handbook* could be written only by Jay.

Reading this book was definitely the most fun I've ever had!

Michele Smith
Host of *American Thunder*

INTRODUCTION

The last Panhead
I built back in 1990.
I love Panheads but
they are too much work.

I remember waking up one evening at around 11 p.m. to the sound of the motorcycles. When I looked out my window, I saw my uncle John and a few friends sitting on their bikes. I was so excited I rushed out of my room and into the front yard. I heard my father and uncle talking, but I don't remember what they were saying because I was awestruck by the chrome.

The next thing I remember was sitting on a gas tank and hanging onto handlebars. As I was ridden around the block, I could feel the warm air rush against my face, the smell of the gas and oil was intoxicating, and the rumble from the pipes, awesome! I was four years old and that was the day I fell in love with motorcycles. Not just any motorcycles, but American-made Harley-Davidsons.

Twelve years later I got my motorcycle license, and six years after that I owned my first Harley. In the late 1980s and early 1990s, I had a few extra bucks and went partners in a custom motorcycle shop in Traverse City, Michigan, with a guy named John Villanueva. Back then if we spent twenty-five grand building a bike, we were happy to sell it for twenty. Needless to say, it wasn't a business that paid the bills

"I fell in love with motorcycles. Not just any motorcycles, but American-made Harley-Davidsons."

but it was fun. John eventually sold the shop and, for all intents and purposes, retired. I have not seen him in many years.

For most of my adult life I have had a career in the entertainment industry, first in music and now in television. During my television days, I have produced major network shows and enjoyed some success. In 2004 I answered an ad in *The Hollywood Reporter* that read: "Looking for producer with motorcycle knowledge." To make a long story short, that was how I became the producer and occasionally an on-air personality for *American Thunder*.

American Thunder is not the biggest show I have worked on, it doesn't pay the most, and it's not the most-watched TV show. However, it is the longest-running, number-one-rated motorcycle magazine show. In 2007 it celebrated its 12th season...that's longer than *Seinfeld*.

Over the last few years, other television networks and producers have created other motorcycle shows and their popularity has definitely influenced the American motorcycle culture. But the original show that first put guys like Jesse James on TV was *American Thunder*.

The American motorcycle culture has always been about authenticity and recently has become watered down by the influence of the media and the influx of new bikers. I hope that this book helps restore that authenticity and you find my experiences over the last 25 years informative, humorous, and straightforward when it comes to a culture that is near and dear to my heart.

My passion for motorcycles grows every day, and I will never forget that night when I was four years old and took my first ride.

John (shown here) built this bike for an actor using my design. This was before every actor in Hollywood owned a Harley.

My former partner John Villanueva in front of our shop, Old Mission Scooters, in Traverse City, Michigan.

"My passion for motorcycles grows every day, and I will never forget that night when I was four years old and took my first ride."

CHAPTER ONE

GET IT STRAIGHT

American Motorcycles

From Rebel to Respectable Overnight

Sometime during the year 2000 the chopper replaced the Porsche as the midlife crisis boy toy.

Why? Simple. TV! TV? What kind of answer is that?

In 2000, a little network called the Discovery Channel produced a show that aired right between shark attacks and the secrets of the pyramids called *Motorcycle Mania* and starred a guy named Jesse James. Was this the great grandson of the famous Wild West outlaw Jesse James? It made sense. That guy rode a horse across the Great Plains, and what did this guy do? He built motorcycles—big custom badass motorcycles, or as most people call them, choppers.

For the first time, millions of God-fearing people who subscribed to a channel devoted to learning and higher education got a glimpse into a lifestyle that for years was regarded as taboo. The Discovery Channel was determined to re-educate us and tell us how wrong we, the American people, were about bikers. All the moms across America were saying to their kids: "Now watch closely and go get your father."

Suddenly, a generation of baby boomers and their children, sitting comfortably on their couches with enough money to afford cable television, were able to confess their secret desire to be a biker: "If it's on Discovery it must be OK!" For the first time ever, women and children watched a well-produced, beautifully filmed show and learned something about men, motorcycles, and, more important, about bikers. They discovered that bikers were generous, interesting people and there was nothing better than that feeling of the wind in your face on a beautiful sun-drenched afternoon.

The Everyman fantasy was validated. It was not only OK to like bikes, but there was money in it. And not only was it a legitimate business, it was very respectable, blah, blah, blah. The image of the scary outlaw biker raping and pillaging was wiped out in one 90-minute Discovery program, and a new generation of bikers was born (or maybe just let out of the cage).

I could go on and on about how every male is born with an inner rebel, but who cares. The fact is that every boy wants a motorcycle from the day he first sees one. And then his father wipes that thought completely out of his head in one nanosecond, but of course this only makes him want it more. For every male in the United States,

"He built motorcycles— big custom badass motorcycles, or as most people call them, choppers."

owning a motorcycle has become a collective pent-up frustration. You know exactly what I'm saying. Every guy reading this is nodding his head and saying, "Yep, that's true."

Now imagine an entire generation of baby boomers who were just left with a big inheritance (by the voice that told them they could never own a motorcycle), sitting with the family watching the Discovery Channel. Yeah, pretty much game over.

The checks and balances in the American motorcycle culture were changed forever just by saying it was acceptable to own a chopper. If that wasn't enough validation, soon after *Motorcycle Mania, American Chopper* aired on the same network, and get this: It was about a father and son who wanted to get closer by building custom choppers! Need I say more?

If you're reading this, it means that you are new to riding, have probably just bought a bike (maybe a Harley), or are thinking about buying one. Your son, daughter, grandson, granddaughter, wife, or someone close to you probably bought this book for you as a present. "Daddy's into motorcycles; he'll love this." Believe me, that's what was said.

If you read the intro, you know I've been riding for more than 25 years and have loved every minute of it. Because there are so many new riders hitting the open road, I wanted to give you, the new rider, some basic guidance so the rest of us who have been riding for years won't hate you. I'm kidding, but only a little. I'd actually like to share my experiences with you, tell you what I've learned, and help you from looking or feeling uncomfortable as you become part of this counterculture. And who knows, maybe even prevent you from killing or hurting yourself or someone else.

The first thing we should clear up is the definition of the word "chopper."

If you think it comes from the long, raked-out front end of Peter Fonda's bike in the cult classic movie *Easy Rider*, you're wrong. But don't feel bad, most people think the same thing.

The chopper was invented, for lack of a better word, right after World War II. Guys coming back from the military had very little money and needed cheap transportation. So the United States government offered to sell them their surplus Harley-Davidson WRLs cheap. Today a restored WRL goes for about $25,000, so if your great uncle Leo has one in the barn, hide this book and offer to take it off his hands.

BIKEOLOGY:
Bobber

"Bobber" is not the nickname you gave your pal Bob in high school. You may also have heard the word "bobber" thrown around a lot when guys talk about old-school bikes with short front ends and narrow chassis. That term came from the same time period as the chopper and simply refers to cutting about a foot off the big, heavier back fender–hence bobbing the fender.

Many vets took advantage of this great deal, and thousands of Harleys flooded the roads almost overnight. However, being guys and being born with the need for speed, basic transportation wasn't good enough. So, put yourself in their position: Here you are with your new military Harley-Davidson and it has everything except the kitchen sink, but you're broke so you can't add any high-performance pieces to make it faster. Still, that need for speed is banging at the back of your skull. Hmm, what to do? Easy. Take shit off. Make the bike lighter. But what happens when you can't unbolt anything else? You have to start cutting off any extra heavy stuff. You're literally chopping your bike up and, bingo, the word "chopper" is added to the dictionary of American pop culture.

"A Chopper Is Not the Main Character in a Horror Movie."

While no one can say for sure, I would guess that at some point while chopping up his bike, some guy chopped off the neck and rewelded it at a greater angle, thus creating a long, raked-out front end. Obviously it looked pretty cool and others followed. Soon, the word "chopper" became synonymous with long stretched-out front ends. Yes, it's perfectly acceptable to call long front-end bikes choppers. Everyone does, but now you know the true origin of the word, and one important thing I hope you take away at the end of this book is that authenticity is key to being part of the biker culture.

The Samurai Versus the Cowboy

A line was drawn in the sand in the 1960s between the guys who rode American-made motorcycles and the guys who rode Japanese bikes. Before you answer which guy you are, here's the difference between the American and Japanese motorcycle cultures.

The guys who came back from World War II ended up owning Harley-Davidsons because, as we've learned, the government made them cheap and available. But what happened when some of these hardcore war vets couldn't find jobs? Their inner rebel surfaced.

In the early 1950s, a bunch of hardened vets who lived in Hollister, California, got together and raced around on their fast, chopped-up surplus Harleys…just for fun. After a few of these meetings, the boys got a little bored and decided that it would be more fun to tear up the town. What that basically consisted of was breaking a few windows, riding on sidewalks, and "catcalling" women. Pretty mild by today's standards, but back then? Look out, it was Armageddon. When the cops got involved and the media heard about it, it was big news. The headlines read: Bikers Terrorize Small Town.

This episode instantly branded bikers (Harley riders) as outlaw renegades, regardless of the fact that the police were also riding Harleys and that Harley-Davidson was an upstanding American company. In one interview, a motorcycle cop said that the Hollister bikers were giving guys who ride a bad name and that it was only 1 percent of Harley riders who were outlaws. Hence the birth of the term "1%er." And, of course,

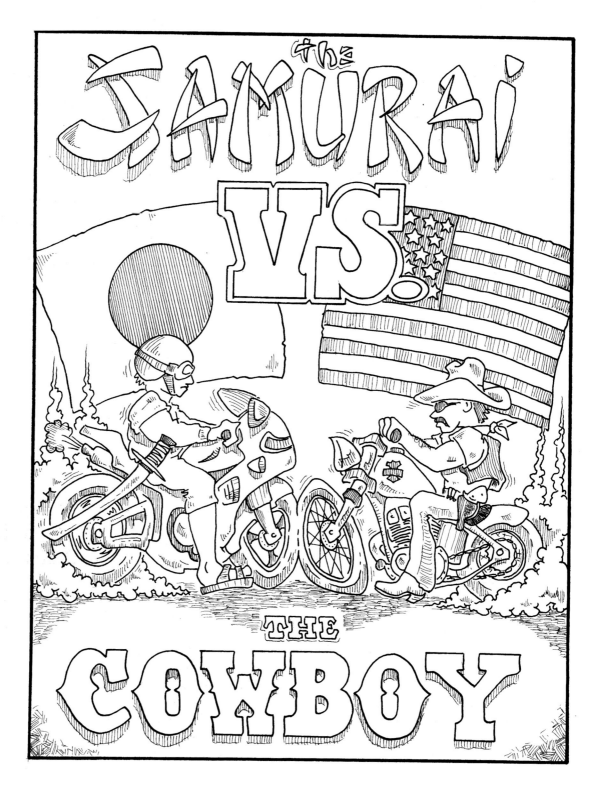

not siding with "the man" (the police) was the macho thing to do. So all these Harley-riding World War II vets wanted to be 1%ers.

These same guys took it a step further and formed what was probably the first motorcycle club ever, called the Pissed Off Bastards. As the story goes, these World War II vets hung out and raced up and down the runway at a military base in California's San Fernando Valley. The locals around the base started saying, "Look at those guys on their motorcycles, they're just like Hell's Angels." They were referring to the group of daring fighter pilots made famous by the Howard Hughes' movie *Hell's Angels*. And this is the unofficial story of how the Pissed Off Bastards became the Hell's Angels.

BIKEOLOGY:

The Japanese motorcycle industry was founded as a result of Harley-Davidson licensing their blueprints, tools, dies, and machinery to the Sankyo Company of Japan.

In 1969, there was a stabbing in Altamont, California, by a Hell's Angel at a Rolling Stones concert. (The Rolling Stones allegedly hired the Angels as security, something that, to this day, cannot be verified.) Regardless, the stabbing incident sealed the fate of bikers as outlaws until that fateful year when the Discovery Channel aired the first *Motorcycle Mania*.

Anyway, because the general population really didn't know the difference between a Harley and a Honda, all motorcycle riders were labeled as bad guys and movies such as *Outlaw Bikers From Hell*, *Easy Rider*, and *The Wild One* fueled the public's imagination.

Because of this stigma, Honda and other Japanese motorcycle manufacturers feared that sales would decline, so they launched an advertising campaign that attempted to clean up the biker image. These ads included young, clean-cut couples in white or light colors, unlike the image of the bearded, black-leather-jacket-wearing Harley riders, and slogans like: "Some people have all the fun."

This ad campaign immediately defined the two sides of the American motorcycle culture, and for 30 years it was a turf war. The American-made motorcycle rider was an outlaw. The Japanese motorcycle rider was a well-respected, clean-cut, law-abiding citizen.

> "The American-made motorcycle rider was an outlaw. The Japanese motorcycle rider was a well-respected, clean-cut, law-abiding citizen."

As the two sides became more and more defined and the two cultures grew further and further apart, a Japanese-made café-style racing bike began winning all of the major motorcycle races in the United States, making the situation even worse.

This war between the two cultures was so real and lasted so long that even into the early 1990s, bar owners at rallies such as Sturgis and Daytona would hoist Japanese bikes up into trees and set them on fire as a symbol against the import motorcycle scene.

The American-made motorcycle, primarily the Harley-Davidson, soon became synonymous with patriotism: "Buy American, support America." This, of course, was all kept highly charged by Harley's marketing strategies. The American bald eagle and American flag practically became trademarks for the company. So associating one's self

A biker's version of a Japanese garden at the Last Resort in Daytona.

with a Japanese product implied that you weren't a true American. Long story short, there was us, the Harley riders, and them, the Japanese motorcyclists.

As the war raged on, Harley began losing ground, and in 1969 Harley-Davidson merged with AMF (American Machine and Foundry). AMF's mission was to make motorcycles part of its already huge sporting line that included bowling equipment, pool tables, and snowmobiles. Unfortunately, AMF was so huge and spread so thinly the motorcycles they were producing suffered in quality. It looked like Harley was about to go out of our lives forever and the Japanese had won.

But (and there's always a "but") in 1981 the founding families of Harley-Davidson and their employees put everything they had on the line and used every penny to buy the company back from AMF. Talk about an all-American Cinderella story.

Once Harley had regained control, leaders vowed to bring back good old-fashioned, American-made quality—and they did.

Harley-Davidson was back in business, investors believed, and the stock soared. Here's the other "but": It still wasn't enough to catch the Japanese sales. So (this is the "so" after the "but") what could Harley do? They had a great product and great new motor innovations, but they had lost too much ground.

Enter the United Sates government for the second time in the company's history. The government imposed a new import tariff on all automotive goods imported from Japan. You see, the American car companies were also losing ground to the

"The American-made motorcycle, primarily the Harley-Davidson, soon became synonymous with patriotism: 'Buy American.'"

Japanese market. Suddenly Harleys and Japanese bikes were much closer in price and the race was on again.

Now, this is where Harley has huge balls. Instead of frantically putting as many new bikes on the street and playing catch-up, it dramatically slowed down production so that customers were waiting up to a year for their new bike. The company claimed that it took more time to turn out quality bikes, and it instantly created a huge demand for the product. Americans stayed loyal to the brand, and that changed the tide.

Once again Harley-Davidson was a major player in the motorcycle arena and began cutting into the dominant Japanese motorcycle market. But that didn't stop the war. The Japanese fought back by launching a V-twin cruiser that looked just like a Harley: the Honda Shadow. For the first time a Japanese bike had a V-twin engine, a trademark that had set Harley apart from all others. So if you own a Japanese motorcycle, what kind of guy are you? Let me answer: a wannabe. You bought a bike from a company that wanted to be like something else. Harley-Davidson was the original. Bottom line. End of story.

BIKEOLOGY:
OK here come the arguments

Japanese bikes are more reliable and Harleys break down all the time:
Bullshit. That was before 1984. Harleys are as bulletproof as any bike out there and have some of the most advanced technology available to the motorcycle industry.

Harleys are too expensive:
Too bad. Owning an original part of history is priceless. Although it's become a lot easier to be a badass biker by simply not shaving for a few days before the weekend and buying a leather jacket, the least you could do is buy an American-made motorcycle and be part of the culture that defined freedom on the open road.

When I was 10 or 11, I remember seeing a photo on my parent's wall. It was of my father and mother standing in front of this huge beautiful red motorcycle. I immediately asked my dad what it was. He said it was an Indian and that was it. Not what year, not how long he owned it, not what model it was. A few years later I figured out it was a Harley-Davidson. When I told my father I knew it was a Harley, he finally 'fessed up. You see, he didn't want me to know because of Harley's bad-boy reputation.

In collective America there was no in-between: If you rode a Harley you were a badass. My dad didn't want me to crave a Harley because he was afraid I would become a thug or an outlaw, and that stuck with me. I had to have a Harley from that day on. No question about it.

When I finally got my first one it was a 1967 XLCH Sportster. I was 20 years old. To own that bike I had to sacrifice dinners with my girlfriend, time with my friends, and more. Why? Because it was a 1967 Sportster.

I basically rebuilt it in my kitchen. I kicked that thing until I almost broke my knee. I used a wire hanger to fix just about everything that would fall off. I pushed it, pulled it, sweated over it, cursed it, and loved it. I knew that year that as miserable and as tough as it was maintaining that bike, I was hooked forever. Hell, the smell of the fuel got me going. The noise it made from the old rusted mufflers was awesome. Everything I had imagined about what a Harley would be like was true. But it was a challenge and sacrifice. I hate guys who cry poor about buying a Harley, or say shit like, "Hey, it's all about the ride." How the fuck do they know? If you want to be a part, even a small part, of something that is exclusive to American history, then shut up and do it right. If you can't afford a new Harley, buy an old one. That's even better. One that breaks down, pukes oil, and makes you miserable trying to keep it running. At least you'll earn respect and you'll be getting into the culture in the right way.

You're either done with this book by now or you're still reading and thinking one of two things: I get it or this guy's an asshole.

Other Brands of American-made Bikes

A V-twin is a bike that has a motor with twin cylinders shaped in a V. This was what made Harley stand out. Now you say, "Well, I see many Japanese bikes with V-twin motors." And you're right, but let's call them metric cruisers. That's the politically correct way the industry refers to them.

This is the second time I'm showing you this photo, but wouldn't you if you had parents this cool?

"... I had to sacrifice dinners with my girlfriend, time with my friends, and more. Why? Because it was a 1967 Sportster."

My 1967 XLCH Sportster right after I completed a year-long frame-off restoration.

Other American V-twin bikes include:

- ☠ Arlen Ness's production line Big Dog Motorcycles

- ☠ Bourgets

- ☠ American Iron Horse

- ☠ Victory.

These bikes are all basically long-front-end, wide-rear-tire bikes. It's what everyone calls a chopper, but you know better now. These are all OEM (original equipment manufacturer) motorcycles. This means that buying one of these bikes is the same as buying a Ford or Chevy or any other well-known vehicle. As opposed to what, you ask? That would be a special construction bike. Those are the bikes that are built in a small shop or home garage.

"Everything I had imagined about what a Harley would be like was true."

I don't recommend buying a special construction bike right away; maybe after a few years on the road and a couple of other bikes in the garage. These bikes take a good bit of knowledge and you could get hurt or killed if Joe Bob Chopper's doesn't torque the bolt in the hub properly. If you do buy one of these bikes (usually a one-off custom is more than $50,000 and I've seen them go for as much as $200,000) and you put it in your collection and never ride it, here's what I say to you:

- ☠ You had better have several other bikes that you ride.

- ☠ You had better be able to at least change the oil in those bikes.

- ☠ You had better at least ride it twice a year for 100 miles just to make sure it runs.

- ☠ You had better not call yourself a biker unless this bike is part of a collection you've been putting together for years and you know the difference between a Pope and an Excelsior.

My point is: If you're an art collector, put this book down and buy a book on art history.

I Want a Bike Now!

So you get it. You're ready to buy a bike for the first time. What do you do? Buy a Harley, right? Wrong! Now you're saying, "What the fuck! This guy has just spent the last several pages telling me about the American motorcycle culture and everything it stands for, so I need to buy a Harley. Right?" Right, but not yet.

This is where the book starts to move away from the history lesson and into the dos and don'ts.

Don't buy a Harley as your first bike. Why? Because you can't ride a 700-pound bike safely the first time out, and you have no idea if you'll like riding. You think you might, but you don't know. Trust me. A few close calls could change your opinion fast.

Pick up the local classifieds and find a Honda, Yamaha, or Kawasaki for about $500 to $800 and not bigger than 750cc. Sign up for a local class that teaches motorcycle safety. It takes a few weekends to complete. You'll get a sense of what riding is all about and you'll know if it's something you want to learn more about. If you feel stupid doing it, you're doing it right.

My first bike wasn't a Harley, it was a Honda 350. My father, who loved motorcycles but hated the image of Harley riders, had bought a Honda 350 when I was 15. Of course I begged, borrowed, and stole the bike every chance I could. My father knew I was going to take the bike, so instead of locking down the proverbial keys to the candy store he told me I could ride the bike, but he laid down a ton of rules. Hey, I'll take rules over a hard "no" any day.

First he taught me to ride in a parking lot on a Sunday morning. He showed me how to accelerate, shift, brake, etc.

Then he let me ride around the block when he was home. Then I could ride around the block a few times when he wasn't home. Then I was finally allowed to ride with him and his friends.

After a few months of practice I was very comfortable riding. The only thing I hadn't done was ride on the highway. So one Sunday morning my dad and I met up with my uncle Al and a bunch of his friends who were all cops. He was and is in a motorcycle club called the Blue Knights. This was my first actual ride in the real world. Only one of the cops had a Harley and my dad was doing everything to discourage me from getting near the guy.

I got on the highway and took the bike up to 60. "Wow, this is cool," I thought. "Scary as hell, but really cool." We rode for about an hour and I loved it. I got it. I was down with it. However, I couldn't stop hearing the guy on the Harley in front of us. I knew which guy I was going to grow up to be.

Then we started heading up Bear Mountain in New York. There were a lot of twisty turns. I just about shit my pants; there was barely a guardrail between me and the

BIKEOLOGY:
Advantages to taking a riding course

☠ You'll get your license quicker.

☠ You'll save on your insurance.

☠ You'll be able to practice.

☠ Some classes even offer the bike, so you won't have to spend a dime before you realize you hate riding.

several-hundred-foot drop off the side, and I was last in the pack. Suddenly I felt this horrible pain in my shoulder, burning searing pain. Fuck, it was a crazy pain, but I couldn't let go of the throttle because of the incline and I couldn't pull over because there was no turnout. Bang! Again the pain started, over and over for about 10 minutes. Finally I got to the top and pulled into the rest area. The guys were all standing around smoking and I was white as a sheet. My father asked what's wrong, and as I tore off my pseudo-leather jacket (I thought it made me look cool) a fucking bee or yellow jacket (or whatever you call the things that can sting you over and over without dying) flew out. After a few minutes of trying to be a tough guy, I got some hiker to give me some bee sting ointment and all was well.

OK, so what's the big deal? A bee stung me. What's the point of this story? The point is I didn't panic. I had been riding around on this little Honda 350 for several months before, and because I was very comfortable riding in general I was able to keep it together instead of jerking the handlebars and going over the edge.

When you ride, shit happens. Bees fly up your jacket, people cut you off, bugs smash hard against your face. Get used to it. You can't be on a 700-pound Harley for the first time and stay safe under good conditions, never mind a bee stinging you in the arm several times while you're riding up a mountain.

Everyone who loves you (and probably the person or family member who bought you this book) wants to postpone seeing you in a coffin. No, you won't be very cool riding around on the piece of shit you bought in the classifieds, but when you're ready to move up to a bigger bike you'll be a better rider. And when it's all said and done that's what matters most.

Also, ride your little piece of shit in the rain—yes, in the pouring rain. If you think it doesn't rain when you're in Daytona at Bike Week with your friends 100 miles out of town, you're wrong. Learn to ride in the rain.

BIKEOLOGY:
Buy a cheap Honda, Yamaha, or Kawasaki for several reasons

☠ You'll need to get used to riding.

☠ You won't be out of a lot of cash if you don't like riding. My brother had the same opportunity and learned to ride just as I did. But after seizing the motor on the Honda 350 and going down on the Kawasaki, grinding off the front of his full-face helmet and breaking his collarbone, he decided that it wasn't for him.

☠ If you get into a funky riding situation (and you will), you'll have a better chance of correcting when going down.

"When you ride, shit happens. Bees fly up your jacket, people cut you off, bugs smash hard against your face. Get used to it."

Narrow It Down

So you really want to be part of the American bike culture. You're comfortable on a motorcycle in a variety of conditions. Now you have to buy an American-made bike. It should be a Harley, but which model?

Sportster

The common mistake first-time riders make is that they immediately buy a Sportster. Bad knee-jerk reaction. Everyone figures that a Sportster is an entry-level bike, and it is, but what most people don't consider is how they fit or look on it.

Here's who should buy a Harley Sportster: Anyone who is less than 5 feet 7 inches and weighs less than 160 pounds. It's that simple. Sportsters are great bikes and they're fast, but you're gonna look like an elephant on roller skates if you're tall, and every guy I meet that has owned a Sportster for more than six months is trying to sell it. The story is always the same: "I grew out of it and want a bigger bike." And Sportsters aren't as smooth or as stable on the highway as the bigger Harleys.

Simply put, a Sportster is not a laid-back cruiser. It's a sports-style bike made for a sporty ride. Ninety-nine percent of guys want to lie way back on the bike, sitting low in the saddle. And you cannot do that on a Sportster.

Now let me just say it out loud. Most riders who buy and keep Sportsters are women. Guys reading this with a tricked-out 1200 Sportster—calm down, it's all good.

"Don't Be Afraid of Buying a Bigger Bike."

Buell

In 1985, when engineer Eric Buell developed this bike with its Sportster motor, he intended it to be a café-style race bike. In 1998, Harley bought a majority share of Buell and has come out with several versions, even an off-road model called the Ulysses. So if you want an American-made sportbike, get a Buell. But remember, even though it has Harley components it's still basically a sportbike.

V-Rod

I don't really think the V-Rod fits in the Harley family. In my opinion, it's not part of the American biker culture because it looks and performs too much like a Japanese import. However, the Screamin' Eagle V-Rod called Destroyer is a kick-ass production drag bike, but that's a whole different category.

REVIEW

☠ You know why every guy in your neighborhood has a Harley in the garage and doesn't shave from Thursday until Monday morning.

☠ You know what a real chopper is.

☠ You know what a bobber is.

☠ You know a little about how the image and culture of the American biker developed.

☠ You know that the Japanese bike builders copied the Americans.

☠ You know what a V-twin is.

☠ You know the difference between an American V-twin and a metric cruiser.

☠ You know what an OEM bike is as opposed to a one-off custom build.

☠ You know that if you're new to riding, you should not run out and buy a Harley-Davidson as your first bike.

☠ You know you should take a riding safety class.

If you can't remember any of this, **reread it** because going forward won't make much sense.

So for argument's sake let's eliminate these bikes as your first Harley:

☠ The Sportster

☠ The Buell

☠ The V-Rod

What's left? Every other bike in the Harley lineup. The choice from here out is very simple. There's absolutely no reason to make this difficult. The first question you have to ask yourself is:

Speed freak or just plain freak: What kind of rider am I?

☠ Do I want to ride alone or with a passenger?

☠ Do I want to go on 300- to 400-mile rides or short weekend day trips?

☠ Do I want to commute to work?

☠ Do I want to do a shitload of customizing to my bike or just add a few little things here and there?

☠ Do I like any of the bikes my friends have?

☠ Do my friends like their bikes? One of the best things you can do is ask guys what they like or don't like about their bikes.

I could go on and on about each Harley model, which has a stiffer suspension, handles better, has bigger bags, etc. But here's what it comes down to: You pick the bike that feels the best when you sit on it and the one that looks right to you . . . period.

Don't become a tech nerd before you even ride the bike

Learning about your bike after you own it is all part of the experience. You'll become infused into the lifestyle. I can't tell you how many times I sat in front of one of my bikes with a biker magazine open planning a new idea, or how many pages I ripped out of magazines with stuff that I thought would look great on my bike. When you own a Harley, it's about discovery.

TIPS:
Finding a dealer that YOU like.

- ☠ Go into your local dealer a few months before you want to buy a bike.

- ☠ Get to know the sales guys and the parts guy. Ask them questions.

- ☠ Don't act like you know everything.

- ☠ Ask how much they charge for labor by the hour. $75 to $85 is pretty fair.

- ☠ See if you can test ride some bikes.

- ☠ If you think the dealership is full of assholes, don't buy your bike there. There are many Harley dealers. It's a pretty good guess that you can find a dealer you'll like within 25 or 30 miles of where you live.

- ☠ Don't buy a bunch of bullshit merchandise before you have a bike. The culture starts with the ride, not the fucking T-shirt.

- ☠ Be sure that you can buy a completely stock bike without any extras forced on you and don't be talked into doing anything custom to the bike until you ride it for a while.

What the hell is a Softail?

Its amazes me how many guys who own a Softail don't know what it means. A Softail is Harley-Davidson's trademark name for a certain type of suspension. The shocks are mounted under the motor/transmission. The shocks are connected to the swingarm, the triangle-shaped piece that connects to the rear tire. The swingarm is connected to the frame with a pivot bolt. This allows the back tire to move up and down independently from the part of the frame where the motor is mounted. The reason they call it a Softail is because back in the early days bikes had no suspension except for the springs under the seat. The rear wheel was bolted directly to the frame, making it rigid mounted, or a hard tail.

The other type of suspension Harley offers is a set of shocks that mount from the fender struts to the swingarm. You see this type of suspension on the Sportsters, the Dyna Glides, and other models.

When buying your first bike, do not get talked into buying a hard tail or rigid

A lot of aftermarket companies offer cheap hard tail frames, but you won't be happy riding one as a first motorcycle. A hard tail is meant for short rides, or as many call them, bar hoppers. More than 60 miles per hour, your kidneys will hate you. However, a hard tail rigid bike is a part of the culture and eventually everyone should own one, but later in your riding career.

Choose the Right Dealer

I remember going into a local Harley dealer in Connecticut when I was a kid and asking about parts for my Sportster. The guy behind the counter was an asshole. Now I know why. Obviously he was a biker who had ridden for many years and I was a snot-nosed kid who wanted to be a tough guy. Back in the day you weren't just accepted into the biker culture because you had a few bucks and a custom bike. Unlike today, you had to earn respect.

When I left the dealer I felt like shit, but I went back the next day and toned down my badass attitude and it was one of the best things that ever happened to me. I realized it was better to be humble, keep my mouth shut, and listen to someone who had been part of the culture for a much longer period of time than I had.

You're probably never going to have the same experience with a Harley dealer like I did some 25 years ago. The guy selling you a bike today is making a six-figure salary, has a family, and is basically a corporate employee. Back in the day most guys who had shops were just about making ends meet, so it was their way or the highway. Think about it. If you were a biker in the 1970s or even 1980s, what profession is opening its arms to accept you? Not many. So you strike out on your own, start a shop, and basically cater to guys with the same personality as you. It's a brotherhood.

The guys who work at a dealer today know more about the product they sell than you probably do, so listen. Do you own research and don't believe everything you hear, but at least listen.

The dealer may try and convince you to:

- Change the pipes

- Upgrade the paint

- Add some chrome

My 1987 softail with way too much shit on it. I actually added more shit after taking this picture in Daytona. Then a few years later I took most of it off.

"I think the total receipts over the years came to something like $32,000."

You will want to do it all, but don't. Wait. I know a ton of guys who put everything on their bike because it looked good on the wall at the dealer. I call that a Frankenstein bike. It's just ugly. You know the bikes: The ones with the giant skulls and long braided things hanging off the handgrips.

It can be an expensive mistake as well. I had a 1987 Harley Heritage and it was sweet. I owned it for 11 years and by the time I was done I had an entire bay of my garage filled with shit that I had bought for the bike and taken off. I think the total receipts over the years came to something like $32,000. The reality is that I could have done it all for less than $10,000.

I bought the Harley of my dreams, now what?

Ride the shit out of it. But before you do that, you're going to need some gear. This could be the difference between looking like a complete poser or someone who actually has some idea of what the fuck is going on.

What you need and don't need

Don't buy everything that has a Harley logo on it like a belt buckle, coffee mug, wallet, boots, etc. There will be plenty of time to sift through the Harley-branded stuff that you really like. The day you buy your bike and the weeks after, you're going to think everything looks great. Relax. Give your family a chance to buy you stuff, because from now until you sell your bike everyone is going to buy you something Harley-Davidson, like it or not!

Here's What You Really Need to Get Started

Helmet

Wearing or not wearing a helmet may be the biggest debate in the world of motorcycles; however, I think it's pretty easy to sort out.

☠ If the state you live in mandates you wear a helmet, then you wear one.

☠ If you are worried about falling off and hitting your head, then you wear one.

☠ If your son, daughter, wife, or mother asks you to, then you think about it. (You probably should wear one.)

I grew up in a state where helmets were not required, but my father made it a requirement if I was going to ride. Over the years I've gone back and forth. Sometimes I wear it and other times, where there's no helmet law, I don't. It's hard to wear a helmet in South Dakota on a 90-degree day rolling down the road. There may not be a better way to experience pure freedom.

"It's hard to wear a helmet in South Dakota on a 90-degree day."

BIKEOLOGY:
The fake brain bucket

This is the helmet that almost every guy wears right off the bat, and it offers zero protection. It's basically just to fool the cops. I even wore one. However, that was before the new DOT-approved half-helmets actually became reasonable to look at.

OK, if you've been riding for several years and got one of these so you didn't look like the Great Gazoo, I get it. But now you can actually buy a DOT one that looks almost the same.

You're a complete idiot if this is the helmet you buy with your first bike. These are novelty helmets; they don't do shit if you crash. They look the same as the new DOT ones, so what's the point? Don't be that guy in his mid-50s, overweight, wearing a polo shirt, Bermuda shorts, slip-on shoes, and one of these helmets. Fuck you guys! Go back to the Porsche.

I will say that lately I wear a helmet more times than not. I'm getting older, there are more cars on the road, and I've seen the consequences of falling even while riding at a slow speed. So let's just say that, regardless, you are going to buy a helmet.

There are basically three types of helmets:

☠ A full-faced helmet. This style has a piece that goes across the chin and covers most of your head and face.

☠ A full open-faced helmet, which is pretty much the standard.

☠ A half-helmet, which is like a policeman's helmet.

The decision to get one of these helmets is ultimately yours, but the full-faced helmet with the chin guard is undoubtedly the safest if you get into an accident. Remember when I told you how my brother stopped riding after he wiped out on my dad's Kawasaki? Well, he ground the face off his helmet, and if it hadn't had full-face protection, plastic surgery may not have been enough to fix him. But because of the helmet, he didn't have a scratch. On the other hand, a full-faced helmet is hot and cuts down on visibility. I personally don't wear one.

A full open-faced helmet is the same without the chin protection. It comes down past your ears and is the most traditional-looking helmet. This helmet provides pretty good protection if you bang your head.

A half-helmet comes down to about your ears. Now, there are some variations on this helmet but it's pretty much half the traditional helmet. Most guys I ride with or see riding opt for this style. It allows at least some protection with maximum visibility and comfort. In recent years, the makers of these helmets have been able to meet the DOT (Department of Transportation) standards for safety and have streamlined the look. Several years ago a friend of mine bought one and he literally looked like the Great Gazoo from *The Flintstones*. Nowadays the style and fit is much better; however, don't buy a helmet if it looks like you're wearing a light bulb on your head. There are plenty of cool safe options out there. I recommend this type of helmet.

Don't get the one that has all the shit painted on it from the manufacturer, like flames or an eagle. You can paint it later. Just get a black helmet and remember you're a new rider. You don't need to draw attention to yourself. Also, don't forget to buy an extra one for your wife or girlfriend.

I like to wear a vintage helmet. You know the crazy blue, red, purple, or even yellow heavily metal-flaked kind that you saw cats wearing in the 1960s and early 1970s. Even that one Peter Fonda wore painted with the Stars and Stripes is cool. They actually made a DOT replica, one that looks like it's from the 1970s. These helmets never go out of style, they make a pretty bold statement, and if you know a pinstriper they look pretty sweet all pinstriped up. But, hey, it's a style thing. You'd better have some confidence if you're going to sport a vintage lid.

Jacket

After the war, Harley-Davidson started selling its own brand of black leather jackets. Why? Because the black leather jacket had become so popular with riders and synonymous with bikers that Harley wanted to capitalize on their popularity by having its own label. Since then, of course, Harley capitalizes on everything. Hell, I have Harley darts. Regardless, Harley makes a really good leather jacket. However, don't buy one with a giant logo or American eagle embossed on it. And do not buy a leather jacket with fringe on it, unless you're a chick.

Keep it simple. Make sure it has either a good permanent lining or a zip-out lining. If it's not a Harley-brand jacket, try and buy one that's made in America. Why? Two reasons: One, it's going to be heavy-gauge leather and have good zippers on it; and two, because it's made in America. See the trend here?

There are two basic styles of jackets: One is a more British racing-style jacket with a short collar, and the other has a snap-down lapel. Either will do. Your jacket will become a part of you. It will go almost everywhere you do, and the older it gets and more weather-beaten the better. Your jacket will become as much a part of you as your bike.

Patches and pins

You're going to want to put something on your jacket as soon as you can, so I recommend collecting patches only. Pins break off. Now this leads me to types of patches. One of the first things a dealer is going to do is convince you to join HOG, Harley Owners Group. It's an organization started by Harley so that Harley owners could get together, ride, share events and news, raise money for

BIKEOLOGY:
The badass leather vest

Do not buy a black leather vest. There's absolutely no reason for it, it doesn't offer much protection, and it's so obviously not cool it's painful. The only guys who should and could wear leather vests are club members. If you're not one, you don't need one.

I bought one about 20 years ago, really nice quality, with Indian nickel buttons. But after one week I realized that it was pointless and embarrassing. It's been in my closet ever since. Every so often I take it out, try it on, and think about where I can wear it. The answer is always the same: Nowhere.

BIKEOLOGY:
Other jackets

When it's too hot for leather, your basic Levi's denim jacket will do; or a long-sleeve Dickies shirt is fine.

BIKEOLOGY:
FTW & DILLIGAF

In your travels to rallies and events you will run across two patches over and over again with the initials "FTW" and "DILLIGAF." Here's what they mean:

FTW: Fuck The World

DILLIGAF: Do I Look Like I Give A Fuck?

BIKEOLOGY:
Swap meet

A swap meet is like a giant yard sale for motorcycle parts. You'll find everything from trash to treasure at a swap meet.

charity, etc. Join if you want, but just keep in mind that it's just a group you pay to be part of. *You are not in a motorcycle club.*

I bring this up because when you join HOG you're going to get a huge 13-inch patch and a few small ones. Throw the huge 13-inch patch away immediately.

There's nothing worse than seeing that patch on the back of someone's new black leather vest, which I already told you NOT to get, as if they were in a motorcycle club. Only real clubs' members wear patches on the back of their vest and it's something they have to earn.

If you're confused about what a real club is, I can tell you that they range from the Hell's Angels to the Bikers for Jesus. All of these club members have one thing in common: They live for the club. This club subculture is so much deeper than just being a biker. It would take me hundreds of pages to explain. Bottom line: These guys are committed to whatever colors they have flying on their back. Being a HOG member does not put you in that category. Just sew the 2-inch HOG patch on your sleeve, get the newsletter, pay the dues, and support your local chapter. Buy a book by Sonny Barger if you want to know more.

As far as other patches are concerned, I like to get one from every rally I attend and group them together. Occasionally I'll find something I like and just put it on for the hell of it. So get a plain black leather jacket and fuck it up over the years. Every time you look at it you'll have a memory.

Gloves

You need them. Get two pairs, preferably made out of deerskin. Deerskin can get wet over and over, stay soft, and not crack. It also dries out faster than leather. Get a regular pair that comes up to your wrist and get a pair of gauntlet gloves. These are the best. They have 3- to 4-inch collars at the wrists that go over your jacket sleeves, which keeps any air from getting in and making you cold. These gloves will make an otherwise miserable cold ride much, much better. It's pretty much science: When your wrist gets cold, it pumps cold blood through your body thus dropping your entire body temperature.

Please, no fringe on the gloves. You're not General Custer. And no cut-off fingers. You're not auditioning for *Rocky Ten*.

Chaps

Yep, you need them. Any style will do. Chaps can get really expensive. I've seen a pair go for more than $5,000 and they were actually very cool. I guess when it comes to chaps you can kind of go for it. You won't have any patches on them. You won't wear them a lot. But when it's cold they're the best things ever.

The best place to buy chaps is at a swap meet or rally. You'll get the best deal and usually they can fit them for you on the spot.

Boots

Need them, too. Black work boots or any work boots are fine. The best makes in my opinion are Chippewa, Carolina, and Frye. These companies make their boots with Vibram oil-resistant soles, which you'll want when you get gas, believe me. There's a lot of slippery shit on the road.

The simplest and most traditional are engineer-style boots. Sketchers even makes a few styles that are pretty cool. Don't get boots with logos on them. Again, overkill.

Rain gear

Definitely! Buy rain gear at the dealer when you buy your bike. Harley makes excellent rain gear. And buy the stupid rubber boots. Trust me.

About 10 years ago I rode up to Laconia from Connecticut. It was a five-hour ride. In June the East Coast weather is completely unpredictable, and being from the East Coast I knew it. However, I was too cool to pack my rain gear. Now, I had been riding for 20 years before this and I assumed I could manage in the rain. I was wrong.

An hour into the ride, the rain started coming down pretty hard. My entire group pulled over and put on their nice heavy rain gear. Me? I was cool. I had chaps and a leather jacket on. How bad could it get?

We pulled out from the underpass and within 10 minutes it was a blinding storm. The raindrops were so big they felt like rocks hitting me. I was completely soaked to the bone. It was so bad that all of the guys in front of me with rain gear pulled over under another bridge. I couldn't see, and I was so wet and my leather so drenched that for some reason (and to this day I don't know why) I just stopped in the middle of I-91. I think I was just so overwhelmed by the storm that I shut down. I'm seriously lucky that a car or worse a truck didn't run me over.

The fact is I was so shaken from the rain and not having the gear, I froze up. Literally. A few seconds later I came to my senses and rode up under the pass where the rest of my group was. We waited out the storm and when it was over everyone took off their gear and were nice and dry. I, of course, had nothing to take off and was soaked to the bone. I rode the remaining three hours freezing. I was sick with pneumonia for a week afterwards.

> **"I had nothing to take off and was soaked to the bone. I rode the remaining three hours freezing. I was sick with pneumonia for a week afterwards."**

The moral of the story: Get good rain gear, bring it with you whenever you travel overnight and wear it when it rains. You're not too cool!

Another tip for riding in the rain is to get a leather bandana for your neck. Put it on *after* you zip up your rain jacket. This way when the rain hits your neck it runs down the outside of your jacket. There's almost nothing worse than being all dry in your gear and rain finding a way down your neck and sopping you underneath. You can also pull it over your mouth and nose to keep the rain from pelting your face.

Eye protection

Eye protection is a must. You might not know this, but it's a mandatory law in all 50 states to wear eye protection when you ride a motorcycle. You'll need at least two pairs of glasses: A pair of sunglasses for the obvious reason, and a set of clears for night riding.

The best styles of glasses are wraparounds, the ones with a thick side to them. These glasses keep the wind out and prevent your eyes from watering. I recommend Arnette or Von Zipper brands. They are expensive (about $100), but they're great and they come in a bunch of styles that work. Oakleys are also pretty good, but are more for skiing. I have also found some of my favorite pairs at the $10 sunglasses kiosks you see in malls or drugstores.

The most important thing is that the sides are wide enough to protect your eyes. Your local dealer will have a bunch of styles that will work, but again, a $10 pair is sometimes as good as a $100 pair and you won't feel as bad when you lose them in a drunken stupor at a rally (and you will).

A very popular style right now is the kind with the foam around the lenses. These are supposed to be the best for keeping the wind out, but I find that they fog up and I can't see shit. I do, however, have a pair of clear goggles that work like magic in the rain. But honestly, it's trial and error. When it's wet, almost everything fogs up. I tried that anti-fog stuff once and it worked okay.

There's nothing more annoying than a bad pair of clear glasses. At night a bad pair of clears will show halos around every light like little rainbows. Glasses with glass lenses are going to be clearer than plastic for night riding. If you can, get a pair of glass lens clears or a pair with scratchproof lenses. You can also get the yellow-tinted variety. I prefer these at night because things look brighter, but they take some getting used to. You'll probably have to buy these at the dealer or a rally. There are always great vendors at a rally that actually have stuff that works, but until you find one, buy your clears at a dealer. Chances are they will be the best you can find right away.

Earplugs

Yep, that's right…earplugs. Why? Well, not because your bikes are going to be so loud that you won't be able to hear. No matter how loud your bike is the sound of your pipes is always behind you, so you won't ever blow out your eardrums. Get earplugs to cut down on wind deafness. That's the whooosssssshhhing noise you hear when you're riding. It can get so bad that after a long ride, if you wear a half-helmet, you might keep hearing that sound for a few hours after getting off your bike. Also, wind noise is distracting.

I wear earplugs all the time, even on short rides. My friends made fun of me for about a year until I convinced one of them to give it a try. Now they're hooked. You can hear your bike, you can hear the cars around you, but you don't get that rattling sound in your head. At times it feels like you're floating. Bottom line: It makes the ride more enjoyable.

Another practical reason to wear earplugs is to lower the chance of getting sick. Without the plugs, air rushes in your ears and finds its way down your throat and into your sinus passages. When it's even a little chilly this can make you susceptible to catching colds, and if you're partying all week at a rally your immune system will definitely be weak. Since I started wearing earplugs, I almost never get sick after long cold rides. Now it's just the cocktail flu that knocks me out for a week or two.

You'll find the best plugs at your local pharmacy. They're in a big bag of, like, two dozen, they cost just a few bucks, and you simply twist them between your thumb and forefingers, making them into little cone shapes, and push them into your ear. You need to keep a lot with you all of the time because they're easy to lose and after awhile they get really nasty.

> "Since I started wearing earplugs, I almost never get sick after long cold rides. Now it's just the cocktail flu that knocks me out for a week or two."

Wallet chain

Yep, you need one. Here's your chance to feel a bit like a badass. A chain that keeps your wallet safely in your pocket is definitely a part of the American motorcycle culture. Why? Before bikes had suspensions they were rigid-mounted. That's when the wheel bolted right to the frame causing a lot of vibration, which, in turn, besides rattling your kidneys, would shake your wallet right out of your pocket.

Today most bikes have a shock-style suspension, but I've still had my wallet vibrate out a few times. So get a wallet chain. The choices for this item are pretty dramatic. I've seen a wallet and chain made by Bill Wall for as much as $6,000 . . . and that's not a typo. Or you can find them at any rally for as little as $20. I have to admit that I kind of dig the badass chain thing so I'm a fashion victim here.

Wrapping it Up

When choosing your *first* Harley we've eliminated:

- ☠ The Sportster, unless you're 150 pounds, under the age of 25, or a woman

- ☠ Any Buell

- ☠ The V-Rod

Get to know your local Harley-Dealer:

- ☠ If you don't feel comfortable with them, find another one.

☠ You must be able to buy a completely stock bike from this dealer.

☠ Don't do anything custom to the bike until you ride it for a while.

☠ DO NOT buy a hard tail or rigid frame for your first bike.

Get the right gear:

☠ Leather vest: NO!

☠ Don't buy everything that has a motorcycle company's logo on it.

☠ Helmet: Yes, DOT-approved.

☠ Jacket: Yes. Black leather, British-style with a short collar or American-style with a snap-down lapel. Don't get the jacket with the huge motorcycle company logos embossed on it and no fringe—unless you're a chick.

☠ Patches and pins: OK, but do not sew your 13-inch HOG patch on the back of anything thinking you're in a motorcycle club. If you must show that you're a HOG member, stick with the smaller patch or pin.

☠ Gloves: Yes, two pairs. One regular and one gauntlet style. Deerskin is the best.

☠ Chaps: Yes.

☠ Boots: Yes. Chippewa, Carolinas, or Frye's engineer-style with Vibram soles.

☠ Rain gear: Definitely!

☠ Eye protection: Wraparound sunglasses. You can find cheap ones at the $10 stand. Clear or yellow lenses for night.

☠ Earplugs: Yes. They cut down on wind noise and help keep you from getting sick. Best deal ever for $2 at your local drugstore.

☠ Wallet chain: Yes.

Me at the beach during Daytona Bike Week, 1992.

Chapter Two

Without Looking Like One

Now that you've got your Harley and all of the shit that goes with it, what's next? First, and I mean it: Ride the piss out of your bike. Then, no matter what I say, you're going to want to do some customizing. All you're going to think about is, "What can I do to my bike?" This thought will become an obsession!

Customizing all started with those WWII vets who chopped their bikes to make them lighter. Since then, no one who owns a Harley can leave it alone, and you shouldn't either. Customizing bikes is a huge part of the American motorcycle culture. But a good rule of thumb is: Don't buy anything custom for your bike until you ride it for at least 500 miles. Let's call it a cooling-off period, just like waiting two weeks after you buy a gun before you can take possession of it.

Customizing your bike should be a reflection of who you are. Don't just do it for the sake of doing it. I mentioned before how I made the mistake of putting everything on my 1987 Heritage except the kitchen sink. Well there are two sides to that story. Yes, it was a mistake to bolt on everything I thought would look good and then take it off when I found something else I thought would look better. I paid for my research in chrome. The thing I did right was having a theme when I started.

Having a theme before you buy your first piece of chrome is critical because maybe you won't want any chrome at all. Confused? OK, what do I mean by a theme? From day one I wanted my 1987 Heritage to look like a 1950s Panhead. I like the retro bikes with lots of chrome, white walls, and especially Panheads. I think the Panhead motor was the best-looking powerplant Harley ever designed. So that was my theme.

Even if it wasn't exactly correct for the period, it had to at least look close. The tank emblems were 1950s styles. I replaced the rocker box cover with replica panhead covers by Exotic Cycles, since they make a bunch of retro-styled heads that fit Evo motors. The paint job was pale pink and black with a turquoise pinstripe, and even though that was never a stock Harley-Davidson color combination, it looked like it could have been. I can't tell you how many times guys at rallies would stand around trying to figure out what year this bike was. OK, so I had a theme. It just wasn't executed very well.

Here are the first two questions you need to answer that will help you come up with your own theme:

☠ Do you like racing and going fast?

or

☠ Do you like style and bling? (In other words the "WOW" factor!)

How you answer these two questions will start you in the right direction. You'll need a few catalogs that specialize in custom V-twin accessories. I suggest catalogs from the following companies: J&P Cycles, Küryakyn, Custom Chrome Inc., Drag Specialties, and Performance Machine.

Oh yeah, this would also be a good time to start subscribing to at least one of the many American motorcycle magazines that are out there so you have a clue about what's happening in the industry. Here's a great way to get several for free: Suggest to your friends and family that a subscription would make a great gift this year. I promise, next to this book, motorcycle rags make the best bathroom reading material ever, and you'll learn a shitload about the motorcycle world. (Pun intended.)

"No one should buy a gun 10 minutes after they get into a beef, and no one should buy custom accessories 10 minutes after they buy a new motorcycle."

If you like racing and going fast, you're going to want to keep things to a minimum. That means not a lot of extra weight or bolt-on shit. Bolt-on shit is the stuff you see hanging on the walls at your local dealer. Instead of spending your money on that stuff, you're going to want to focus on motor upgrades. So the first thing I recommend is ordering whatever Harley upgrades are available direct from the factory so the parts are guaranteed and the work is done by a trained pro. Any motor upgrades are going to take a lot of labor, money, and time. And yes, you can upgrade a fuel-injected motor to get big horsepower. I could get into hundreds of pages on how to hop up your motor, but that's not what this book is about. If you're serious about speed and big horsepower, you'll find a way to make it happen.

However, there are two things you should do regardless of how you answered the questions: Change your pipes, and add a breather kit with new jets for your carb or re-map your EFI (electronic fuel injection) system to work properly with your new pipes. By doing these two simple things, you'll increase your horsepower by as much as 10 to 20 percent, and your dealer should do all of this work so it's guaranteed and done right. No matter what style or theme you decide to go with when you're customizing your bike, these two upgrades are a definite and an easy way to increase performance. The pipes you choose will basically set the theme of the bike. Pipes are one of the most noticeable components, and from just one look at the pipe you can get an idea of what the owner of the bike was going for.

Here's what I mean:

A two-into-one exhaust system is perfect for a Pro Street drag race—styled theme:

☠ A pipe comes off each head and goes into one main muffler.

True duals are great for nostalgic styling and big baggers:

☠ This system consists of two separate pipes, one from the left side of the bike and the other from the right side.

Straight pipes work well on bobbers and old-school setups:

☠ Like the true duals, this system consists of two separate pipes. The difference is that both pipes come out on the same side of the bike. They can be together, staggered, or upswept. Think of the choppers you probably saw in the 1970s while sitting in the back of the family's Country Squire station wagon.

Loud Pipes Save Lives

Despite what you might have heard, it's not the pipes that make a bike loud. It's the baffles or lack of baffles. Now, the saying "Loud pipes save lives" is true. Why? Simple. Other vehicles can hear you coming and you'll increase the other drivers' awareness. There's nothing I hate more, especially in California, than when a quiet little crotch rocket bike splits the lane and scares the shit out of me. I would much rather hear someone coming and be prepared. However, loud pipes also get you tickets. So the key is to get a set of pipes that have a good throaty sound, but don't blow your eardrums.

Also, it's not true that straight pipes help your horsepower. Actually, what happens with straight pipes is that you kill all of your backpressure, which reduces horsepower. You might think it's cool to sound like a badass and piss off the neighbors, but it's not a good idea for your bike and you're definitely going to get pulled over.

There are plenty of pipes that will give you both great performance and sound for whatever style you choose to go with for the theme of your bike. Here are my three favorite companies that have the best of both worlds: Vance & Hines, Sampson, and Supertrapp.

"There are two things you should do regardless: Change your pipes, and add a breather kit with new jets for your carb or re-map your EFI (electronic fuel injection) system to work properly with your new pipes."

TIP:
You have to start somewhere so make it here.

One of the best bikes you can buy as your first bike is the Harley-Davidson Softail standard because it's a blank canvas. In other words, this bike has a minimum amount of chrome and extras, and it's also one of Harley's lowest-priced models.

The suggestions I could make to customize your bike would be infinite, but regardless, the key is to have a complete plan before you get started. Once again, do not just pick shit out of a catalog or off the dealer's wall that you think looks cool.

TIP:

Turn off your gas, open your gas petcock and unhook the gas line, and drain it into a 5-gallon gas can.

BIKEOLOGY:
Tin

The sheet metal on a motorcycle is often referred to as tin.

Here are two styles of customizing you can do quickly and relatively inexpensively using a standard Softail

Hot Rod Retro: $2,500 to $3,000

☠ Change the bars to mini ape hangers (not more than 16 inches).

☠ Hide all of the wires inside the bars so nothing is showing. (You should do this always.)

☠ Replace your stock mirrors with round ones.

☠ Install a lowering kit and drop the bike about 2 inches. (You might have to have this done at a dealer because it's a little tricky.)

☠ Put on a set of staggered straight pipes with baffles. You could also use upswept pipes and/or heat wrap them.

☠ Replace the stock air cleaner with one with a round traditional Harley-Davidson style.

☠ Replace the seat with a solo spring seat or just remove the back of the stock seat pad. (The stock seat comes in two parts and you can take the back pad off.)

☠ Get a Phantom pad with the suction backing if you plan to take a passenger for a ride.

☠ If you get a quick-release backrest setup for your bike, you can ride solo or take a passenger. Harley makes the best quick-release backrests, luggage racks, and windshields in the business. You can literally install them in 30 minutes and then take them on and off in 10 seconds.

☠ Replace the plastic chain guard with a chrome one, and make it the smallest one you can find.

☠ Take off the plastic license plate bracket and replace it with a side-mount license plate kit with the light built in.

Paint

Take off all of your tin, that means your front fender, tanks, and rear fender. It's not that hard to do. For a real hardcore look, you can leave your front fender off permanently, but if you ride in the rain I don't recommend it.

Take all of your tin to your local auto body paint shop. Elaborate custom paint schemes are a big part of building a show-quality bike, but I've seen $400 paint jobs on some of the most beautiful bikes. Going to your local paint shop is a great way to get a custom look quickly and inexpensively.

Tell the painter that you want a solid black paint job with *a matte clear coat over it*. The matte clear coat gives it that primer look, better known as flat black or suede. Do not just paint your tin with a black primer. It will look like shit later and it won't hold up. Using a black base coat with a matte clear is just like a regular paint job and will last forever, almost. This should not cost you more than $500.

This part is a little tricky: You need to find a pinstriper. Your local body shop and painter should know one. Do a white and red pinstripe on the sides of your tank and on the tops of your fenders. I leave it to your discretion, but don't overdo it. This should cost no more than $150.

Now put everything back on your bike.

BIKEOLOGY:
Powdercoating

Powdercoating is a powder that is sprayed on and then baked to a matte or gloss finish. It can be done in almost every color.

If You Want to Go a Little Further, for About $1,500 More

Replace the tires with thin whitewalls, have your rims and hubs powdercoated red, and have the wheels re-laced.

Also powdercoat the lower legs on the front forks, derby cover (the round disc on the primary), ignition cover, shift rod, headlight housing, and turn signal housings.

Replace your horn with a vintage-style round horn.

I could go on and on, but this will give you a very cool hot rod–inspired custom bike and believe me, it will look like you spent a lot more money than you actually did.

A Pro-Street Custom: $2,500 to $3,000

A pro-street look might best be described as a low, lean, race-inspired bike. Pro-Street is a take off on Pro-Stock. Pro-Street means street racer. Using the same basic Harley-Davidson Softail Standard as we did for the retro customization, here's how to get a pro-street look:

TIP:

Harley-Davidson offers a chrome swap program that allows you to trade your stock switches, brakes, calipers, and even your Fat Boy wheels for chrome replacements.

☠ Change your handlebars to a set of pull-back drag bars, with a new set of 4-inch risers. This will keep the bars from banging into the tank.

Mike's 1996 Bad Boy after powercoating most componants. Unfortunately these black-and-white photos don't do it justice.

☠ Hide all of your wires inside your bars.

☠ Replace your stock mirrors with a set of thin, narrow, billet aluminum mirrors.

☠ Replace all of your switches with chrome.

☠ Install a lowering kit and drop the bike about two inches. Again, you might have to have this done at a dealer.

☠ Install a two-into-one exhaust system.

☠ Replace the stock air cleaner with a Küryakyn Hyper Charger Pro R. (This will also help increase your horsepower.)

☠ Remove the back of the stock seat, get a Phantom pad with the suction backing for your passenger, and get the quick-attach backrest setup. (Same process used in building the bobber.)

☠ Replace the plastic chain guard with chrome.

☠ Take off the plastic license plate bracket, replace it with a lay-down taillight setup and license plate holder, or do a side-mount plate. But unlike the retro look above, get the vertical mount setup with the L.E.D. light built in.

Paint

Drain your tanks, remove all of your tin, and take it all to your local auto body shop. (Same process as above.) Tell the painter that you want a solid paint job with a rally stripe down the middle of the gas tank. The stripe should be about 3 inches wide with quarter-inch pin stripes on each side of that. A few nice color combinations include red and white, cobalt blue and white, orange and white, and tan and black. Only stripe the tank. This paint job will run you about $600.

If You Want to Go a Little Further, for About $2,000 More

☠ Replace the spoke rims and wheels with a set of billet or chrome mags.

☠ Get a bunch of chrome covers from Küryakyn. The company makes great quick, easy, bolt-on stuff and there's a cover for just about everything. The beauty behind chrome covers is that it's less expensive than taking off the original pieces to have them chromed, there's no down time, and you can do it yourself either all at once or over time.

TIP:
Replacing wheels can be expensive. If you can find a set of used Harley-Davidson mags and have them powdercoated or chromed, this will save you a bunch of money.

☠ You can also powdercoat your derby cover and ignition cover the same color as your paint scheme to enhance the race-inspired theme.

☠ Change all of your turn signals to the small billet ones so they don't stick out very far.

As you can see, even though we've used the exact same bike and the actual

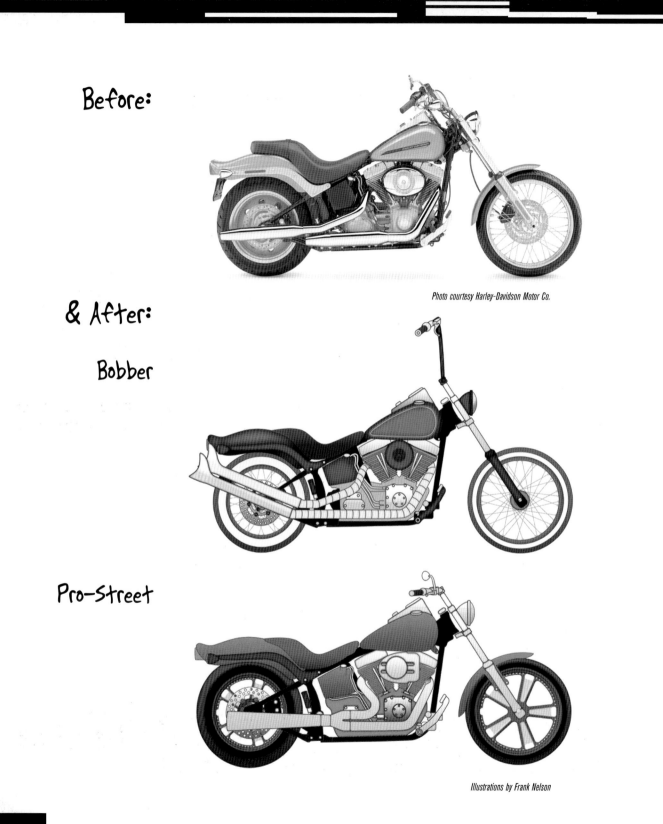

Before:

Photo courtesy Harley-Davidson Motor Co.

& After:

Bobber

Pro-Street

Illustrations by Frank Nelson

labor involved is similar, the final results are very different. The Retro Hot Rod is matte black, has very little (if any) chrome on it, and straight pipes. The Pro-Street has a bright-colored paint job with a rally stripe, lots of chrome, and a two-into-one exhaust system.

Here's What I'm Trying to Get into Your Head

Have an idea, theme, or style for your bike before you buy any aftermarket components. Customizing your bike will cost money, but it doesn't have to break the bank if you plan accordingly. As I said before, I spent something like $32,000 on a bike that I could have done for about $8,000. A few small details can make a radical difference. You can achieve the look you want without wasting a bunch of money if you plan it all out ahead of time.

Start slowly. Some of you may be saying, "Man, $4,000 to $8,000 is a lot of dough!" And in the scheme of life, it is. But not in the world of the American biker culture. I promise you, the most dead-broke guy in the world with a Harley or any American V-twin will spend his money on the bike before paying his electric bill. Your bike becomes your priority. That's just part of the scene.

If you're into this for the practicality of it, get out now or buy a Honda. As you immerse yourself deeper and deeper into this culture, you'll see bikes that have more than $100,000 invested in them.

BIKEOLOGY:
Piece of shit

"Piece of shit" is what you call your bike the minute anything goes wrong.

A perfect example of how it's done right

Over the years I've seen tens of thousands of custom bikes, but the one that stands out in my mind as the smartest and best looking for the least amount of money and labor is my friend Mike's 1996 Harley-Davidson Springer Bad Boy.

As my friends and I spent countless dollars on our bikes (mostly on impulse buys), Mikey sat back and watched. I wondered what the hell he was waiting for. I mean, his bike was still stock after three months. So one day I asked him, "Hey, what's happening with your bike?"

He simply replied, "I'm powdercoating everything." I was bewildered.

"You're not buying new covers or that new chrome thing?" I asked. "What color are you powdercoating everything?"

He replied simply, "Black."

"If you're into this for the practicality of it, get out now or buy a Honda. As you immerse yourself deeper and deeper into this culture, you'll see bikes that have more than $100,000 invested in them."

I was baffled. Now remember, this was before Harley-Davidson came out with the Night Train, which is basically an all-black Softail with almost no chrome. So when Mike told me he was powdercoating everything, I had no idea what the hell he was up to.

That year, when Daytona rolled around, we all met up at Mike's office/warehouse in New Jersey to load our bikes onto a U-Haul truck for the drive down to Florida. Suddenly, it all made sense to me. There it was . . . the coolest bike I had ever seen. The entire bike was powdercoated black, with tan-colored tin. The other really smart thing about Mike's design was that he took into account that the stock frame, hoses, and cables were already black. The results were amazing. How he did it and what it cost was even more amazing.

Picture this: Five guys standing around with their $30,000 chromed-out custom-painted bikes, which, by the way, pretty much all looked the same and way overdone. And then there's Mike's bike.

Most bike builders didn't really start taking full advantage of powdercoating until about 15 years ago because powdercoating was used primarily for industrial machinery. So if powdercoating is cheap, durable, and you can get it in almost any color, the question is: Why

"Anyway, here's what Mike did.
He took all the simple stuff off the bike himself. . ."

use paint? The answer is simple. A powdercoated finish will never have the same depth or shine as paint, and paint is still the only way to go when you want airbrushed graphics. But remember, regardless of whether you use paint or you go with powdercoating, it's all about planning, planning, planning!

My friend Mike obviously took his time to really think about what he wanted to do to his bike, while the rest of us frantically spent money on shit that looked good on the dealer's display wall. Hell, I was so amped up to have a custom everything, I would have bought a brand-new horn cover in black if I could. I never would have even considered powdercoating something like a stock horn cover. Duhh!

Anyway, here's what Mike did. He took all the simple stuff off the bike himself, the tanks and both fenders. Then he took everything to a local powdercoat shop.

He purchased a vintage-style hinged fender, a tombstone-style taillight, and a few other small bullet lights. He took the sheet metal to the local painter and had him spray everything one color, think coffee with cream in it. Sounds boring, right? Wrong!

So here's how much I guess the total project cost him (and I'm guessing because, to this day, it would kill me to know how little he really spent for such an awesome custom):

BIKEOLOGY:
H-D

The initials H-D really stand for "a hundred dollars" cause that's what you'll spend every time you buy something new for your bike.

- ☠ $1,000 for the paint and powdercoating

- ☠ $1,200 for the new bars, rear fender, shotgun straight pipes, and a few miscellaneous lights

- ☠ $400 for a new seat

- ☠ $600 for an S&S carburetor

- ☠ $750 for a little motor work

- ☠ Total: $3,950

"Every time you have the uncontrollable urge to run to the dealer and spend money on the latest greatest new accessory you just saw in a magazine or on a TV show, ask yourself this question: does it work with the overall styling of my bike?"

Almost no labor costs were incurred. (See again, planning ahead.) Mike knew that everything he wanted to do to the bike he could do himself. So when everything came back from the painter and powdercoater, he just bolted all the parts on the bike with no fabricating, extra wiring, or re-drilling holes. And to this day, his bike attracts a crowd.

In 2003, when I first started producing motorcycle television, I had to go to Laconia, New Hampshire. I flew from Los Angeles to New Jersey to meet up with Mike and the boys. Mike let me borrow the Bad Boy and I rode it more than 600 miles to and from Laconia. It was perfect.

Moral of the story

Every time you have the uncontrollable urge to run to the dealer and spend money on the latest greatest new accessory you just saw in a magazine or on a TV show, ask yourself this question: does it work with the overall styling of my bike? The same philosophy holds true when you buy your bike. If you like the laid-back old-school look, don't buy a Fat Boy and then replace the solid mags with spoked wheels . . . know what I mean?

The worst accessory, regardless of your style

There are tens of thousands of aftermarket accessories you can get for your bike, and if you don't pay attention to anything I have said in the customizing section of this book, here's one thing you should remember: No matter what style of bike you have in mind, there is no design that will work with the eagle-claw kickstand.

Holy shit! This product wins my award for the tackiest accessory ever invented. There is absolutely no motorcycle that can look good with a chicken leg and claw as a kickstand in my opinion.

The only product close to this freakish thing is the exhaust pipe with naked girls wrapped around it. I actually saw this product on a bike when I was producing a show for FOX. The bike belonged to the first winner of *Joe Millionaire* and that pretty much says it all!

BIKEOLOGY:
Rube

A rube, or "rubbie," is a rich, urban biker, a person who tries to buy his way into being a biker without making the effort to be authentic.

Have a Custom Chopper?

I wasn't going to get into the dos and don'ts of buying a custom chopper, but if you have to have the long front end and a wide rear tire, these are all good first bikes: Big Dog, American Iron Horse, Thunder Mountain Custom Cycles, Bourget, and Arlen Ness.

Go online, look up these companies, spend $30,000-plus and forget about becoming part of the culture—you've just bought your way in and you're officially a rube (rich, urban biker). Now close this book, and thanks for playing.

Don't get me wrong. At this stage of my riding career I would own any one of these bikes. However, I feel, as I think a lot of us do, that you need to graduate into bikes like these. These eight words might say it best: "If I have to explain, you wouldn't understand." You've seen the T-shirt, and it honestly sums up the entire culture.

"Spend $30,000-plus and forget about becoming part of the culture— you've just bought your way in and you're officially a rube. Now close this book, and thanks for playing."

When you can't figure out what you want, check out the pros: Six completely unique bike builders

1) Arlen Ness

Arlen pretty much changed the custom motorcycle world with his innovations and style. Go buy *Arlen Ness: The King of Choppers*, by Michael Lichter. Check out the bike called *SmoothNess* and the year he built it and you'll get a pretty good idea of what this guy has done for the industry. You can also go visit Ness Enterprises in Dublin, California, just south of San Francisco. It's an amazing 70,000-square-foot motorcycle museum and facility. 🏍

SmoothNess. Photos by Michael Lichter

2) Roland Sands

Roland Sands is one of the youngest of what I consider to be master builders in the industry. Roland literally grew up on a motorcycle. His father, Perry Sands, founded Performance Machine more than 35 years ago.

Performance Machine is one of the greatest success stories I've ever heard. Perry got married and immediately quit his job, much to the dismay of the family, because he wanted to build brakes for motorcycles. With a single drill press and a few limited tools, he made one brake caliber for a friend. When he sold that caliper, he took the money and built two more. The rest, as they say, is history.

To make a long story short, Roland became entrenched in the motorcycle culture. He started racing and, in 2002, after winning two of his last four races and setting two track records, he retired and his dad set him up as a designer working for the family business.

Roland excelled at this position, and he not only became responsible for about 70 percent of the designs that came out of Performance Machine, but he also began building custom bikes to show off the new products. Most of these two-wheeled gems are race-inspired, so if you like the "go fast" look, check out Roland Sands Design or Performance Machine and you'll get some great ideas for your bike. Specifically, check out the bike he calls the *Hard Way*. It's a tribute bike he built to honor his dad's work ethic.

3) Jesse Rooke, Rooke Customs

In 2001, Jesse Rooke broke the mold for how the custom chopper was "supposed" to look with his outrageous Schwinn-inspired *Kali Kruiser*... Jesse is the perfect example of how the Discovery Channel show *Motorcycle Mania* changed the industry for the better. As Jesse was watching the show, he saw Jesse James riding to Sturgis, and he said, "Shit, I can do that!"

Check out Jesse's work if you like a race-inspired minimalist look.

Kali Kruiser. Photo by *Casey Kiernan/caseykiernan.com*

4) Indian Larry

Larry Desmedt (affectionately known as Indian Larry) passed away in 2004 after doing his famous stunt called the Iron Cross. Larry would ride standing on the seat of his motorcycle with his arms extended from each side like a cross. Larry owned a shop in Brooklyn, New York, called Gasoline Alley, which was renamed Indian Larry Legacy after his death. Larry's bikes are the epitome of old school. Most are kick-started, spoked-wheel choppers with hand-fabricated Springer front ends and narrow chassis. If you like the bygone years of American motorcycles and traditional styling, take a look at his bikes for your inspiration. His best friends Paul Cox, Bobby Seeger Jr., Elisa Seeger, and Keino now run the shop.

Daddy-O.
Photo by Bob Seeger, Jr.

5) Chica's Custom Cycles

Chica is from Japan and knows more about the spirit of the American motorcycle culture than most Americans. Sometimes it takes an outsider who is objective to the culture to really get to the heart of things. Chica is difficult to understand at times because of his heavy accent, but he doesn't need to say a word once you see his bikes. Again, like Larry he puts the "old" in old school. Between Larry and Chica you should be able to get plenty of ideas if you dig the 1950s-, 1960s-, and early-1970s-style bobber look.

Rumbler. *Photo by John Wyckoff*

6) Russell Mitchell, Exhile Cycles

Russell had a radical idea for styling a bike and never looked back. His bikes are completely unique in the industry. Russell does what I consider a very industrial *Mad Max*–looking bike. As he likes to say, "You can get any color as long as it's black."

Russell's bikes are beefy, clean, and appear to have no extras on them. However, it's the intricate details that you don't see that make his motorcycles truly exceptional. Russell's brushed satin finishes combined with the matte black paint schemes put Exhile Cycles in a category all by itself.

An Exhile chopper.
Photo by Jim Gianatis/fastdates.com

Out of the hundreds of talented builders I know, these six guys illustrate what I swear by. Have a look in mind before you just start adding shit to your bike. Plan everything and have a goal in mind. That's the key to a successful custom job—not the amount of money you spend.

If you were to line up one of each of these builders' bikes side by side, anyone would be able to see the difference. That's what this culture is all about: Your own personal style and ideas.

Once you start researching the above six builders, you're going to discovery many others with this same philosophy. In my opinion, what defines a master builder is not that he can fabricate a motorcycle on a television show, but that he has the insight and patience to be a *master planner*. When you start to customize your bike, think about how an architect designs a building. Before the construction company breaks ground, it has an exact blueprint of what the final building is going to look like. And it doesn't matter whether you're planning to spend $500 or $5,000 on your bike.

Review

☠ For speed, go with a factory Harley upgrade at the dealer.

☠ Buy your bike stock!

☠ Have a style in mind for how you want your finished bike before you buy any accessories.

☠ Just because it looks good on the dealer's wall doesn't mean it will look good on your bike.

☠ Pipes and paint make the most dramatic difference.

☠ Powdercoating stock parts is a very affordable way to get a custom look.

☠ You don't need to spend a lot of money to get a custom look.

☠ Don't rush out and buy a $30,000 custom chopper for your first bike.

☠ Research well-known builders for ideas on how to get the look you want.

Now hopefully you've learned a little about how the American motorcycle culture started. And you've also learned how not to sound like a complete poser, because you've ridden around on a small bike and now can deal with any riding condition or circumstance. You've chosen the Harley that best suits your personality and style, bought the appropriate riding gear (minus the giant embossed eagle leather jacket) and you've at least started to think about customizing your bike after a well-thought-out plan. *Now what?*

Chapter Three

PLANNING A TRIP

This Time It Doesn't Mean Finding the Guy with the Best Dope

Friends, Romans, Countrymen . . . Stick with Friends

Riding with friends is great, but it can also be very frustrating. Most of the guys I hang around with got into the motorcycle scene about 10 years after I did. And when they did, my first thought was "Man this is great, my best buddies and I will be cruising around and having a blast." Well, what I didn't know was that my pals had a speed problem, and I don't mean meth.

The first time I really had the chance to cut loose on a trip and ride with these guys was in 1992 at Daytona Bike Week, which is a whole other story coming up in a later chapter. Shortly after we arrived in Daytona, we hopped on our bikes and, literally, within the first two minutes, everyone was gone. When I finally caught up to them, they said they were just excited and that they would slow down. OK, I got that. So we jumped on I-95 to head out to Iron Horse and this time, within 10 seconds, they were gone again. What the fuck! Well, to make a long story short, I played catch-up for the entire trip and still do to this day.

Now here's why it's frustrating when the guys you are riding with pull that shit. The guy at the back (usually me) has to race like hell to play catch-up, which is not really that fun. For example, let's say someone gets 200 yards in front of you doing 70 miles per hour. You need to go 75 miles per hour just to even up with them. If you slow down just a little and they speed up just a little, the gap widens and you'll have to go faster. The whole thing just sucks!

I can remember riding down the highway all pissed off because I couldn't find my friends. Eventually I would see them on the side of the road finishing a smoke right by our exit. The entire time I played this game of catch-up and worried about not getting lost rather than enjoying the ride.

If you think I'm whining, try this scenario: You're in Sturgis for the first time. Everyone you're riding with takes off, and suddenly you find yourself alone cruising

"You're in Sturgis for the first time. Everyone you're riding with takes off, and suddenly you find yourself alone cruising down some backroad. It's pitch black, there aren't any streetlights, and you don't know where you're going . . . not fun."

down some backroad. It's pitch black, there aren't any streetlights, and you don't know where you're going . . . not fun.

It's gotten so bad over the years that the guys stuck a sticker on my helmet that says, "I'm so far behind I think I'm first." A few years later I said, "Fuck it" and rode like a wild man to get out in front of these maniacs. It didn't help. They just got in front of me and stayed there.

My point is that when you're with your friends, stay together, slow down, and enjoy. Johnny "Chop" Vasko, a guy who defined being part of the American motorcycle culture and passed away long before his time, once said, "Life goes by pretty fast at 85 miles per hour."

If your friends don't want to ride within your comfort zone, there are a few things you can do:

☠ Make sure you're not riding so slow that you're a hazard.

☠ Pick several meeting points along your route that everyone agrees upon before you head out.

☠ Keep a map with you. Most rally organizers give away maps for free, and they're excellent.

Playing catch-up for years will only piss you off and ruin what could have been some great rides.

How to Keep it Together

When you're riding with a group on the freeway, ride in a staggered formation:

☠ One guy to the left of the lane, and one guy to the right of the lane about a bike distance apart, repeated.

☠ Use hand signals as well as your turn signals when you can. This will give the riders farther behind, who may not be able to see your turn signals, the heads up as to which way the group is heading.

☠ If you're leading the pack, don't make any sudden or radical moves that the group can't make as a whole. Just because you can pass a car safely doesn't mean the bike behind you can.

☠ You're the leader. The guys behind you are looking to you to make good decisions so they don't wreck.

☠ Remember, if the guys behind you are looking at you, they might not see everything that's happening in their immediate area.

☠ A bad leader can actually lead someone right into a problem or accident.

Them's the Brakes

Bikes don't stop like cars. Obvious, right? I promise you, you'll forget, trust me. You need at least two to three car lengths between you and the car in front of you to be safe. Again, make sure you apply this safety tip even when you're leading a group, because if something does happen to you and you go down, or have to make an evasive emergency move, the guys behind will have time to react and not pile up.

Even after 25 years of riding, I occasionally get an unpleasant reminder of this fact. About a year ago I was cruising down the 405 in Los Angeles on a friend's brand-new Fatboy. It was a clear Sunday morning but there was a lot of traffic so I pulled into the car pool lane. (In California, motorcycles can legally drive in the car pool lanes.) The average speed was about 75, so I went with it, even though the regular lane to my left was at a crawl.

So there I was, chugging along thinking how great it was that I wasn't sitting in traffic. Suddenly, about 200 yards ahead, I saw a Mercedes convertible hit the brake lights, but I didn't think anything of it. First mistake.

I should have knocked it down a notch just to be safe. (Down shifting is a critical part of slowing down, combined with proper braking.) But no, I had been in a hurry to get where I was going and smug about passing all of the traffic.

As I approached the Mercedes at full speed, I quickly realized the car had actually come to a full stop, but I still didn't give it much thought. Then, about 75 yards away, I saw the woman in the passenger seat standing, facing me, waving her arms frantically...*bang*! I got it.

In a panic, and without thinking, I locked up the front and back brakes and the bike went sideways. After about five seconds of laying down rubber, I realized I needed to get off the brake and off the throttle and steady the bike or I was going down. My reflexes and experience finally kicked in and the bike straightened out. I came to a stop about a foot from the back bumper of the car. Close call and, as I've said, I've been riding for 25 years.

What Does this Reinforce?

First: *Pay attention to all of the road conditions around you, regardless of the lane you are in.* I should have known that if the lanes next to me were at a crawl, it was inevitable that my lane was going to slow down dramatically. Anticipation!

Second: *Every day I rode my little Honda 350 when I was 16 paid off because there's no way to talk yourself down from 75 miles per hour while your life flashes before your eyes.* It's all reflexes at that point!

Third: *Bikes don't stop like cars!*

A Few Stupid Things to Avoid

TIP:
Proper braking means applying 70 percent of the pressure to the front brake and 30 percent to the back brake with slow, even pressure.

☠ Don't forget to put your kickstand down when you're getting gas. Sound ridiculous? Not so much. I've seen guys pull into a gas station trying so hard to be cool or so stressed out from riding that they stop their bike and just step off to pump their gas and the bike falls over. It's stupid, embarrassing, and expensive. I think this happens so much because for most of your adult life you've been driving a car, which doesn't require a kickstand.

☠ Turn on your gas before you start riding. The first thing to check when your bike starts to sputter or stall is that your gas is turned on. This happens to the most experienced biker. I can't tell you how many times I cursed my piece of shit for breaking down only to realize that the gas was off.

☠ Make sure you have gas before you hit the road. Nothing pisses me off more than getting into a groove with some buddies and then one of them signals that he needs gas.

☠ Speaking of piss, take one. The ball busting you'll receive for the rest of your life for making everyone pull over five minutes into a ride to piss will be relentless.

☠ Bring an extra jacket or heavy shirt with you, along with a pair of clear glasses. Even if you don't think you'll be out after dark. There is nothing better than knowing that you'll be warm and able to see on the way home.

☠ If you drop something, or if something falls off your bike, or if you see the guy in front of you drop something, leave it behind.

Once again, this brings to mind my pal Mike. One year during Daytona Bike Week, all of the usual suspects were heading to a little bar called The Other Place. One of the guys dropped a pack of cigarettes on A1A. Mike saw it happen and decided to make a quick U-turn to pick them up, and he's one of the safest riders I know.

Upon making the U-turn, a cab was in the process of passing a car in the other lane, and because Mike was in the middle of his U-turn he didn't see the cab. *Crash!* The cab hit him broad side. Mike went down, and it was an ugly scene. The bike was mangled. Mike was lying face down, spread eagle, in the middle of the road. From the looks of it we assumed the worst.

Once the initial shock wore off, I ran over to where Mike was lying and said, "Mike, Mike, you're OK! You're fine," even though I wasn't even sure he was alive. Slowly he lifted his head and asked, "How's my bike?" Happy to hear that he was conscious, I replied, "It's fine, bro, its fine. Don't worry about it." Then he looked right into my eyes and with a hint of sarcasm said, "If I'm fine and my bike's fine what the hell hit me, a cloud?"

That's when I knew he was going to be OK.

The ambulance rushed him to the hospital, and of course we all stood around like expecting parents to hear the prognosis. They released him with a bruised kidney and a prescription for some rest and a heat pack. We took him back to our house, propped him up in a chaise lounge chair by the pool, wrapped him in a blanket, and continued to party. (Mike stayed in the chair.)

Mike's bike was totaled, so the best thing that happened from his accident was that it forced him to buy a new one. That bike was the 1996 black powdercoated Bad Boy I talked about earlier.

TIP:
Don't try to pick up anything you drop or see fall off a bike. Instead, try to avoid hitting it and consider it gone.

You've mastered riding with friends and you've hit a few of the local day rallies around your town or city. What's next? Next is the best part of becoming part of the American motorcycle culture: it's time to head out for a multi day trip to a major rally. Rallies may be the best way to get a real slice of the biker lifestyle. The major three are Laconia, Daytona, and Sturgis.

I strongly suggest that you only go on these trips with friends you really like and trust. Why? Because there are a lot of things that can go wrong:

- *You could end up in jail for a night.* That's a good time to have a friend or two responsible enough to get you or give you a few bucks to get out.

- *You could have trouble finding affordable accommodations.* So I strongly suggest planning any of these trips with friends who won't flake out and leave you holding the bag for a lot of money.

- *Go with guys who like to do what you like to do.* For example, if you like to ride all day and get up at the crack of dawn, don't go with a bunch of guys who want to hang out

in a bar all day and sleep till noon. There's no wrong or right way to spend your time at a rally, but I promise you'll turn what could have been the time of your life into a nightmare if everyone wants to do something different.

☠ *Go with guys who can bring about the same amount of spending money you can.* Nothing will ruin a friendship faster than feeling like you're always picking up the tab or mooching off your buddy because you can't afford to hang out. I have friends who I will never go on a bike rally with just based on this one fact.

☠ *Never make it a co-ed trip.* It's either all or nothing. If you're single, don't go with guys who bring their wives or girlfriends.

If You Already Live in a Trailer, Skip this Section
You have your group together so now you have to decide on accommodations. There are three primary options for any trip:

☠ Camping

☠ Staying at a hotel

☠ Renting a house

Camping
Camping is probably the most affordable and most rugged way to live at a rally. Every rally will have several campgrounds available where you can pitch a tent or park an RV. Campgrounds tend to get pretty crazy. Besides the obvious weather-related issues, there are some pretty big noise issues. They don't make a soundproof tent. There are also some sanitary issues. Most campgrounds don't have the greatest bathroom or shower facilities, and even if they do, after a few days they're pretty shitty, literally. However, if you decide to camp out you will definitely party nonstop.

Mike, a day after he was hit by the cab.

In Sturgis, one of the biggest and most well-known campgrounds is Glenco. It's right across from the Full Throttle Saloon about 5 miles out of town. In 2005, I revisited Glenco and took a drive through just to see how it's changed over the years. I wasn't surprised to see that it's pretty much the same as it was in 1996 when I first checked it out. There were hundreds of empty beer cans strung up in trees and lining the pathways. Naked people who should not be naked roamed around on little Honda

We convinced the cab driver to pose for this picture the night after Mike came back from the hospital. At first he thought we were going to kill him.

Left to right: Me, Darryl, Scotty, Ray, Mark, Ronnie in front, Mike on the bike.

50s and golf carts. A multitude of laundry hung between campsites and, well, just weird shit everywhere.

It truly is a makeshift city with tens of thousands of people spread out over miles. It's also very possible to get lost among the trails and tents that extend deep into the forest, which can be a bit scary. On the flipside, I also saw million-dollar campers and buses set up. So don't think camping is just about saving money. It's about the experience.

Staying at a hotel

Hotels are hotels. I don't think I have to explain what that's like. This option can cost you anywhere from $150 a night to several hundred a night, depending on the location. I've done the hotel thing several times and the advantages are simple: Your room is always clean, you can sleep when you want, and you don't have to worry about the weather. But if you stay on the main drag, for example in Daytona, noise will be an issue. I recommend this option if you're traveling with your wife or girlfriend. For big groups it's kind of a drag because you can't really all hang in one guy's room. That gets a little weird.

I also don't recommend sharing a room with more than one other guy. You think four dudes might sleep anywhere, but it won't be any fun with more than two guys in one room.

TIP:

Book your hotel as early as possible, like four to six months in advance. Otherwise you'll get screwed on prices and end up staying 40 to 50 miles out of town.

No matter what anyone tells you, it's better to stay as close as you can to the center of the rally. Once you start staying far away from the origin of the event, it loses its flavor. In Daytona, guys will say it's fun to stay two hours away in Orlando. Bullshit. Save the Disney World trip for the kids. In Sturgis, people like to stay an hour away in Rapid City. I think that sucks too.

"When you hit Sturgis, stay in the town of Sturgis or within 20 miles. It's around Main Street, the Main Drag, where you'll really get the feel for the history and the authenticity of the event."

If you go to Daytona Beach, stay near the beach. Chances are it's the beginning of the riding season for you and you've been cooped up since fall. There's nothing better than the smell and sound of the ocean on an 80-degree Florida day after a long winter.

When you hit Sturgis, stay in the town of Sturgis or within 20 miles. It's around Main Street, the main drag, where you'll really get the feel for the history and the authenticity of the event.

The best reason to stay near the action is that you will absolutely want to go out at night, and there's a good chance you'll drink. I've literally stayed at hotels within walking distance to Main Street in Sturgis and Daytona and it was great. I could hang out all night and walk back to my room. I know what you're saying, "Rallies are for riding so why would I want to walk or take a cab home?" Save the riding for the days when you're sober. There are a few reasons for that besides the obvious ones, like not killing or hurting yourself or someone else.

Oh yeah, and if you do decide to stay and party when your hotel is 50 miles from town, good luck finding a cab that will drive you back. And if by chance you do find a ride, how are you going to get back to your bike the next day? For that matter, where are you going to leave it? The best idea is to stay within cab distance of the main drag so you can lock your bike after a good day's ride and then go drink and party without worrying about the consequences.

A view from the pool table out to the beach. As you can see it was a great place to watch bikes pass by.

Renting a house

Ahh! This is by far my favorite option. The local people in towns where major rallies occur literally move out of their houses for a week to allow big bad bikers to move in. Of course, all of these homeowners have found out over the years that most bikers are good people and will treat their property with respect. Homeowners in these towns understand the economic value of renting out their house for a week. A house in Sturgis goes for $5,000 a week, the same in Laconia, and $6,000 to $8,000 in Daytona. So if

TIP:

The best idea is to stay within cab distance of the main drag so you can lock your bike after a good day's ride and then go drink and party without worrying about the consequences.

you consider that $5,000 to $8,000 could very well represent up to, if not more than, 20 percent of a person's income, it's a pretty good deal for everyone.

The first year I went to Daytona Bike Week in 1992, I wanted to rent a house but had no idea how or if it was even possible, so I called the chamber of commerce and got the name of a real estate agent. Today if you want to rent a house you just get on the Internet and you'll get every option you could ever hope for. I told the real estate agent at the time that we were five guys who were willing to spend whatever it took to stay somewhere nice. I really had no idea how much that was going to cost, but I knew that we wanted to be on the beach.

The realtor quoted me $3,500 for the week. In 1992 that was a lot of bread, right? Nope. Do the math: $3,500 divided by five guys comes to $700 a head. Now divide that over six nights and it comes to about $116 a day.

"Today if you want to rent a house you just get on the Internet and you'll get every option you could ever hope for."

When I recommended renting a house to other guys, they pretty much thought I was crazy. Their initial reaction was, "$3,500 a week! Way too much." They got hung up on the total and didn't divide up the costs. Actually, renting a house is the best bang for your buck.

Once my friends understood what a bargain they were getting, we continued to rent that same house for 10 years straight. The homeowner was so happy with the way we took care of the place, he never even changed his rate. So picture this: It was on the beach, with five bedrooms and three full bathrooms, a pool table, a Ping-Pong table, an in-ground pool, and a huge two-car garage. I can't tell you how many great nights and parties we had there. No really, I can't tell you.

This is the front of the house just off A1A.

TIPS:
When you rent a house:

Hanging around the pool are Ronnie, Mark, Darryl, Mike, some girl, and me the day after Mike got hit by the cab.

☠ Ask for a garage for obvious reasons.

☠ Find out if you need to bring your own towels and linen. Try not to. It's a pain in the ass.

☠ Make sure they have a washing machine and dryer.

☠ Make sure the homeowners clean out the refrigerator before you get there. You'll need a lot of room for booze.

☠ Find out about the phone situation and if you can use their home phone. Cell phones don't always work in these remote places.

☠ Beware of long gravel driveways. I had a friend wipe out on one pretty good once at a house we rented in Sturgis. It could have been the two cases of beer that he was carrying on the handlebars that did it, but the gravel driveway didn't help.

☠ Find out *exactly* how many beds and full bathrooms there are.

☠ If there is a pull-out couch, it's the perfect opportunity to cut a break for the guy with the least amount of cash.

☠ Send the real estate agent a few hundred extra bucks and see if he or she will stock the place with booze and food. Several years ago our agent did this for us and it's awesome to get into town and not have to worry about hitting the grocery store, especially when you're on your bikes.

Me, loading the truck in Daytona.

Chapter Four

TIME TO GET GOING,

But How?

There are four ways to get you and your bike to a rally

- ☠ Be a tough guy and ride.
- ☠ Be a queen and travel in comfort.
- ☠ Don't tell anyone how you got there.
- ☠ Blame everything on your job, money, or your ex-wife.

Be a Tough Guy and Ride

Riding is obviously the purest way to go to a rally, but for most of us with busy schedules it's not going to happen. Shit, motorcycles are my passion and livelihood and I still don't have the time to ride to the big rallies.

If you are going to ride to a rally, there are a few things you should consider. You'll have to figure out how to pack a week or two of gear safely, which could be a real challenge if you don't have a bagger. You have to be prepared for bad weather, especially if you're riding anywhere from the north to Daytona. In March you may even have to deal with snow. There's a chance, and I mean a good chance, that you'll have a mechanical problem with your bike along the way, which means you'll need extra cash and tools. Again, a packing issue. And finally, in my opinion, the best reason *not* to ride to a rally more than 500 miles away: By the time you get to the rally, you'll probably have to turn around and immediately drive back home.

Don't believe me? Let's do some math. Say you're riding to Sturgis from California and you have 10 days planned for your entire trip. That's probably a pretty nice chunk of your annual vacation time. To power through the 1,200-plus miles

"You want to ride from California to Sturgis, you'll need at least two weeks."

Albert and Mark
burned up and burned out
a day after riding out
to Sturgis from New Jersey.

in three days, you'll have to ride for about 10 hours a day—and that's regardless of bad weather or mechanical breakdowns. Plan on taking four days to ride the 1,200 miles—that will still be some serious hours in the saddle. On the fifth day, and I don't care who you are, you're beat up. and you'll need to rest. Now if you're staying in a campground, good luck because you're not going to get any sleep. Hell, you'll have to set up the minute you arrive just to get comfortable and there goes day five. That leaves you one day to check out Sturgis before you have to ride four days back home.

If you want to ride from California to Sturgis, you'll need at least two weeks (14 days). OK, let's see how that works out.

On day six you're ready to check out some of what I consider to be the most beautiful scenery in the country. To hit Mt. Rushmore, Devils Tower, Custer State Park, Deadwood, and maybe the Badlands, you'll need to ride about another 1,000 miles. Not so bad, right? That's only 200 miles a day for five days. (Don't even think of partying all night if you want to keep up with this pace.)

On day 10 the adrenaline is gone. You're exhausted and it's time for the four-day ride home, ready or not, good weather or bad. Let's say you make it home on day 14. Do you think you're going to feel like jumping back into your everyday grind? You won't.

"To hit Mt. Rushmore, Devils Tower, Custer State Park, Deadwood, and maybe the Badlands, you'll need to ride about another 1,000 miles."

Again, I live, eat, and breath motorcycles, and after half that time on the road I need to hide out for a day or two. Oh yeah, and remember, you just used up two weeks of your vacation time. See how the wife and kids appreciate that.

The first year I went to Sturgis was in 1996 and I rode 1,200 miles in five days. The plane ride home was challenge enough. One year—I think it was 1997 or 1998— two of my friends (brothers Mark and Albert) had the bright idea to ride out to Sturgis from New Jersey and meet the rest of us there. We were already there for two days before we even heard from them, supposedly they were about 100 miles out of town and were going to meet up with us later that afternoon. Not wanting to sit around and wait, the rest of us took a day trip to Spearfish. On the ride we saw these two guys blow by us all burnt and beat up, looking really bad. We pulled over for a smoke and someone said, "Hey that was Mark and Albert, wasn't it?" I looked at him and thought, "Dude, we're in Sturgis. There are 500,000 bikes on the road. There's no way."

We finally got back to the house we were renting and sure enough, there were Mark and Albert sitting in the garage waiting for us. It was them who had flown by us on the road; talk about an unbelievable coincidence. But what was even more unbelievable was the way they looked. They were sunburned three times over, peeling, and completely dehydrated.

That night they told us all about their great adventures. They had been on the road for five days, which basically added up to riding all night and breaking down in the middle of nowhere. They were pumped and full of adrenaline. The next morning they realized that in less than 72 hours they were going to have to ride all the way back to New Jersey, and suddenly the glamour of riding out to Sturgis was gone. I have to make one comment here about having guts. Albert did the whole trip on a Sportster that he had bought a week before.

So, with the thought of riding all the way back to New Jersey, dead tired, in three days, they made a little change of plans. They bought two one-way airline tickets to Newark and found a bike hauler with extra room on his truck to ship their bikes back. It wasn't cheap. *Do you see what I'm getting at?*

OK, So You Want to Ride Anyway

Here are a few things you should do:

- ☠ *Get your bike serviced two to three weeks before you leave.* Don't let your bike sit all winter and expect to ride it hard for a few thousand miles without having any problems.

- ☠ *Go with at least one other person.* Riding alone isn't that great an idea.

- ☠ *Pack a basic tool kit.* Harley sells a complete kit for a few hundred bucks that will be easy to carry on your bike. Add duct tape, bailing wire, and a can of flat-tire sealer to the kit.

- ☠ *Bring a cell phone and check in with someone along the way to let him or her know where you are and where you'll be next.* You don't want to end up in a ditch bleeding out for two days before anyone knows you're missing.

- ☠ *If you don't have saddlebags, make sure you have a backrest on your bike and purchase a luggage bag made especially for a bike.* (Küryakyn makes a lot of good ones and so does T-Bag.) These bags are basically luggage for your bike. The larger styles of these bags attach to your backrest and have safety tie-downs engineered to keep them securely fastened to your bike. I suggest you get the biggest one that will fit on your backrest and a smaller one that attaches to your handlebars. You'll use these bags for as long as you ride, so they are worth the investment.

- ☠ *Plan a route in advance and bring maps.*

- ☠ *Plan gas stops.* My friend Albert from New Jersey did his trip to Sturgis on a Sportster, so planning accurate gas stops was critical because his tank capacity was significantly smaller than Mark's bike.

- ☠ *Plan rest stops in hotels or motels, and stay on the first floor so you can park your bike in front of your room.* When you stop for the night, bring all your bags and any other easily stolen items into the motel room.

- ☠ *Bring a chain lock and a disc lock, and when possible lock the bikes together.* Security will be crucial, since your bike is all you have on the road.

- ☠ *Drink a lot of water every time you stop and piss every time you stop.* The wind and heat will drain your body of moisture. Stay hydrated.

Be a Queen and Travel in Comfort

This is a pretty realistic way to get to a rally and there are several ways to accomplish it. *You can throw your bike in the back of a pickup truck.* The only problem with this option is that you need an extended bed with a ramp to get the bike in and out and someone to help you load and unload. So if you're going to a rally with your wife or girlfriend, she had better be pretty strong.

The better option is a trailer you can pull behind your car or truck. However, you'll need to buy or borrow one. There are several excellent models that fold in half when you're not using them and take up very little room. I strongly suggest that if you do buy a trailer, make it the kind that can haul *two* bikes, not just *one*. You can always haul one bike on a double trailer, but you can't haul two bikes on a single trailer.

If you're really going to do a lot of traveling, you should also consider a covered trailer, maybe even one with a small fold-down bed in it. But again, you'll need a place to store it when you're not on the road. The companies that make these covered trailers usually have a variety on display at rallies so you can get a good idea of all of the options available.

Don't order a trailer sight unseen. Check it out in person and ask a lot of questions. Hauling a trailer all over the country does take getting used to, so get a good one that you feel comfortable towing.

You can also rent a trailer or truck from Ryder or some other rental company, but you have to check their rules and regulations about hauling a motorcycle. For several years my crew and I rented a 24-foot Ryder truck, put in a plywood subfloor with eyehooks, and packed seven bikes in the back. Economically, it seems like a pretty good idea, right? The gas and cost of the truck whacked up seven ways and came to about $500 to $600 per person. That was okay but it

TIPS:
If you want to trailer your bike:

☠ Make sure your vehicle can pull the weight of your trailer and bike(s).

☠ Do not cover the bike with a tarp. Leave it exposed. If you cover a bike when you're in an open trailer, dirt will get trapped under the cover and scratch it. Also, the tarp can blow loose and the ends can scratch it. Let it get dirty and deal with cleaning it when you arrive.

☠ Empty the gas tank to a half-gallon or less. A full tank may spill over the sides and ruin your paint.

☠ Use soft tie-downs so you don't scratch your chrome and paint. Secure the tie-down straps to the lower triple tree and fork tube (less chance of snapping the bars). Use a block of wood under the front of the frame; this keeps you from blowing out front fork seals. With the block of wood you are putting the hold-down pressure on the frame and not the fork seals. Make sure no wires or lines are between the wood and frame.

☠ Tie off the loose ends of the tie-downs so they don't blow around and scratch the bike.

☠ Use two people when loading and unloading.

☠ Park the trailer and the ramp on as level ground as possible or, if you can, get the trailer lower than the ramp. This is when you'll wish you paid attention in physics class.

☠ Make sure the ramp is dry, made for a motorcycle, and has a grip surface so the wheels don't slip.

A view from inside the truck that me and the guys used to haul our bikes from New Jersey to Florida, with all of the bikes loaded—there were some scratches, I believe.

took two days for my friend Mike to build a subfloor with eyehooks and loading the bikes was a pain in the ass.

The second year we all made the trip, we decided based on the experience we had the previous year that two guys would drive the truck and the rest of us would fly, but that wasn't without its hassle either. It was March in New Jersey. The night before we left it snowed. While we were pushing the bikes up the oading ramp one slipped, fell over, and the eyehook in the subfloor punched a nice 3-inch hole through the outer primary, which in turn caused all of the oil to pour out. This really could have screwed us up big time. Remember, five of us were flying down two days after the truck was supposed to leave, so any delay would have meant five guys in Daytona without bikes. Not good.

In a desperate attempt to get the bikes on the truck, we woke up a local Harley mechanic at midnight. He was able to somehow snag a new primary and then spent three hours replacing the damaged piece so the truck could get on the road. I'm glossing over all of the fighting, arguing, and expense caused because I think it's pretty obvious how five guys felt standing around at midnight in a freezing cold snowstorm looking at the possibility of blowing a big bike trip. The fact was that we were just lucky to overcome the situation.

That's not the only disaster I've had loading a bike

One year I was loading my bike and found I didn't have a ramp, so I used a big old piece of wood about 4 inches wide. Well, it was drizzling a little and the piece of wood was too short so the slope was pretty steep. However, I figured I'd been loading bikes for years and I had my brother-in-law Morgan helping me out so it would be no problem. I figured wrong.

I rolled on the throttle, let out the clutch, and Morgan pushed the bike from the back. This worked well for about two seconds. The front tire made it onto the truck, but the back tire came off the shitty wet wooden ramp and I fell. As I started falling, my hand was in just the right position to crack the throttle wide open and I couldn't let go.

Picture this: The back tire of my freshly chromed-out painted Heritage is spinning at full speed. I'm wedged between a fence post and my bike trying desperately to keep it upright so it doesn't crush me. My poor brother-in-law is asking me what to do and, oh yeah, the rain has turned to snow!

Somehow I managed to get my leg on solid ground, hit the kill switch, and balance the bike, which was now teetering on the lip of the truck, while Morgan held up the back end.

To Morgan's credit, I have to say, he came through in a pinch and most likely saved me from serious injury. However, right before we started the fiasco he had expressed

his concerns and my bravado reply was *"No problem. I do this every year."* To this day every time I ask him for help, no matter what it is, his smart-ass comment is "No problem. You do this every year, right?" So, for no better reason than not having your brother-in-law bust your balls for life, use the right ramp when loading your bike.

Tips for Doing it Yourself:

- *Make sure your bike is in gear when you secure it.* A bike in neutral will move around and loosen the tie-downs.

- *Make sure the kickstand is down.* In case the bike does come loose, it will land on the kickstand. I can't tell you how many times I've pulled over to check a bike and found the tie-downs loose, but the bike safely on the kickstand.

- *Check the tie-downs at every stop and check the bike in general in the rear-view mirror to see if everything looks OK.*

- *Try not to get into too many situations where you'll have to back up long distances; you'll know why the minute you do it.*

- *Always use a safety chain on the hitch to the towing vehicle.*

- *Load and unload your bike while the trailer is hooked up to your vehicle.* If you try to hook it up after the bike's already loaded, there's a chance that it will roll forward and the hitch will do some severe damage to your bumper and then some.

- *If you're loading two bikes, make sure there is enough room between each one so they don't bang together.*

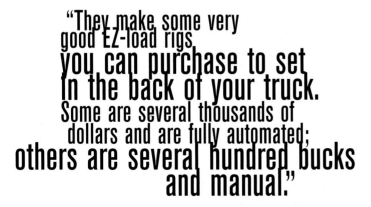

"They make some very good EZ-load rigs you can purchase to set in the back of your truck. Some are several thousands of dollars and are fully automated; others are several hundred bucks and manual."

- *If you're loading the back of a pickup truck, use a really long safe ramp or park on the down side of a hill, again physics.* They do make some very good EZ-load rigs you can purchase to set in the back of your truck. Some are several thousands of dollars and are fully automated; others are several hundred bucks and manual.

- *Don't throw anything else in the bed of your pickup or trailer if it's not secured in place.* You don't want shit sliding around banging into your bike.

☠ *When you get to your final destination, find a parking lot close to where you're staying and unload there.* There's nothing worse than a guy unloading in the hotel parking lot or on the side of the road blocking traffic.

☠ *Beware of mud, soft dirt, grass, or gravel.* You'll lose your footing.

Don't Tell Anyone How You Got There

This means shipping your bike and flying to a rally. Oh, I can hear it already: "Shipping your bike is for rubes." *Let's review a few things first before you jump to conclusions:*

☠ You only have a limited time to spend at a rally, so if you drive you'll eat up at least several days.

☠ There are lots of things that can go wrong on a drive and eat up even more time.

☠ There will be plenty of riding once you get to a rally.

"There's no doubt that with the extra cost of the plane ticket, this method will cost more on paper than if you rode or towed your bike. But I rationalize it like this: You'll have more time at the rally, and getting there and back will be painless."

As I said before, if you're within a few hundred miles, riding or trailering is the way to go.

With that said, I think shipping your bike and flying is the most cost-effective method of getting to a rally. After hauling bikes down to Daytona several times with a bunch of smelly cranky guys, I said to myself, "There must be a better way." Coordinating several guys' schedules, the gas, and splitting the driving is a real pain in the ass.

As I said before, I actually calculated the cost of hauling your bike yourself and it was close to $500 per guy, and that's without calculating our time, the wear and tear on the extra vehicle we brought (because six guys will not fit in the cab of a U-Haul truck), and the time to load and unload all of the bikes. It's not a bargain.

In 1995, I decided that I would look into a motorcycle shipping company. Back then there were only a handful of truckers specifically set up to haul bikes. After some research I found a guy in Tennessee.

It sounded simple and, as it turned out, it actually was. Here's how it worked: The five guys and I who usually travel together dropped off our bikes at one central location two weeks before the start of the rally. Then a truck came and picked them up. The cost

was $500 per motorcycle, there and back. Two weeks later we all met in the airport, got on the plane, and in a few hours we were in Daytona. Once there, we rented a car and drove to the house we were renting, and within a few hours all of our bikes were delivered. Perfect!

After a few years of using this transport company we became friends with the owner, Randy, and occasionally he would hang out with us during the course of the rally. On one particular night we were sitting around with a few young ladies, all of us pretty drunk and trying our best to be tough guys. Randy, who by his own admission is the poster child for the definition of redneck, wanted in on the banter. So as the BS flew, one of the girls looked at him and said, "Randy, you have really nice teeth." Almost on cue, Randy smiled, reached into his mouth and pulled out his full set of dentures and asked if she would like a closer look. She nearly passed out. We couldn't stop laughing. What this has to do with shipping your bike, I have no idea except that it was funny as hell.

My point is that several years ago it was a bit challenging to get a company you could trust to haul your bikes, so this option was a little scary. To Randy's credit he never even scratched a bike. At one point he even offered a detail service for an extra $50.

There are a lot of companies that offer this service. One company does an exceptional job and I used them in 2004: Daily Direct (www.haulbikes.com or 1-888-Haul-Bikes). These guys will pick your bike up at your door. They never ride your bike, their trucks are impeccable, they are fully insured, and they check every detail on your bike before they load it and unload it. The cost is about $700 for almost anywhere in the United States.

There's no doubt that with the extra cost of the plane ticket, this method will cost more on paper than if you rode or towed your bike. But I rationalize it like this: You'll have more time at the rally, and getting there and back will be painless.

TIPS:

A few things to know if you ship your bike:

☠ You'll have to part with it two weeks before the actual event and wait two weeks after the rally before you get it back. Any company that ships bikes needs a few weeks to make all of the pickups and drive the truck to the event.

☠ Use a reputable company that specializes in hauling motorcycles.

☠ Make sure you have only a half-tank of gas before they load it. Most companies will tell you how they want the bike before they load it, but this will also ensure that the gas doesn't spill over the top and ruin your paint.

☠ That's about it. For a few extra bucks you'll have peace of mind, enjoy the entire time you spend at the rally, not be burned out from the ride, and most important, not have to ride home after partying all week, which might be the most compelling reason.

Blame Everything on Your Job, Money, or Your Ex-wife

Another option is to rent a bike at the rally.

Because of my job as the producer for *American Thunder*, I'm always guaranteed a bike at a rally from either a friend or someone in the business who wants my opinion of how the bike performs.

In 2005 a few friends wanted to come to Sturgis with me and didn't want to worry about shipping their bikes. So I looked into the feasibility of renting bikes for them. I must admit it worked out well. The main drawback of renting a bike is obvious: *It's not your bike.* Several years ago I couldn't even fathom this method. I wanted nothing more than to ride and show off my personal bike while cruising Main Street. However, after attending 15 years of rallies, this isn't that important to me anymore. Honestly, I'm getting a little lazy, but more importantly I'd rather enjoy the ride then then to show off.

The process to rent a bike is simple. Go to any rally website and look at the rental options. If, by chance, you can't find any rental places on the rally websites, look for Harley dealers in the surrounding areas and call them. Chances are they're renting bikes for rally week or have information on who is.

In 2005, my friends Darryl and Paul rented bikes for the Sturgis rally. They rented the bikes at a Harley dealer in Gillette, Wyoming, five minutes from the airport. Then they rode an hour through beautiful roads into Sturgis. They did the same thing on the way back. We tried to do this the next year, but for some reason the dealer had decided not to rent bikes anymore. So I called Rapid City Harley-Davidson and found that not only were they renting Harleys, but they had an affiliate program with a Harley-Davidson dealer from out of state that was trucking in several dozen more bikes. This worked out even better. Both Paul and Darryl flew into Rapid City, grabbed a shuttle from the airport to the dealer, and were on the road within the hour.

> "Renting bikes also gives you **the opportunity to try out different bikes** that you normally would never get a chance to ride."

Renting bikes also gives you the opportunity to try out different bikes that you normally would never get a chance to ride. Both Darryl and Paul rented Road Glides with full tour packs, and they thought it was great. Having a nine-foot chopper or a hot rod bobber is cool, but not always practical. These Road Glides had luggage packs, radios, farings, etc. They held all of our jackets, chaps, glasses, T-shirts, etc., with no problem.

The cost to rent a bike was around $125 to $150 a day with a three-day minimum. So it's very cost-effective when you weigh that against shipping or hauling it yourself.

Pack it In

Packing for your trip might be one of the most important things you can control. When I went to my first big rally in 1992 it was to Daytona Beach Bike Week and I packed everything under the sun. Not really smart. Over-packing isn't a big issue if you trailer your bike. However, it is if you're shipping or renting a bike. Why? Because when you get off the plane and have a big bag with you, how do you get it and your bike to wherever you're staying?

The first time the guys and I flew to a rally and had our bikes shipped, we got off the plane, collected our huge duffel bags, and stood around feeling stupid. None of us thought ahead about how the hell we were going to carry our luggage on our motorcycles to the house we rented. Eventually we paid a shuttle driver $50 to drop off the bags at our house, but that wasn't so great because we ended up sitting around for hours waiting for him to show up. There is a better way.

Your Friend's Father's Duffel Bag from the Korean War Just Won't Do

The best way to ensure you, your luggage, and your bike all go together is to pack using a T-Bag or a Bag Tech bag from Küryakyn. Both companies make several styles of bags that can hold a day's worth or a week's worth of clothing and gear. These bags fit safely on a motorcycle and double nicely as luggage you can carry or check on a plane. Küryakyn actually makes a bag with roller wheels that can be pulled. I strongly recommend you purchase at least two styles of bags, one for week-long excursions and another for overnight trips.

When you buy your bag, check that it fits properly on your bike before you travel or that it will fit on the bike you rent. Several models fit with a backrest and several don't require a backrest at all.

I mentioned that you should eliminate your passenger seat when you customize your bike, so now you're saying, "Hey, I don't want a bag sitting on my back fender" and you're right. To solve this problem I recommend a Phantom pad. Again, you can get these from Küryakyn. A Phantom pad works on a suction cup system. It simply sticks to your rear fender and becomes your passenger seat. Now, with a detachable backrest (which I also recommend when customizing your bike) and a Phantom pad, you can convert your bike from a solo setup to include a passenger and carry any piece of motorcycle luggage in minutes.

Don't Pack Like a Woman . . . Unless You are One

Years ago I would get so excited about hitting a rally that I would pack and repack months in advance. But over the years I have learned the hard way, as with everything

"I strongly recommend you purchase **at least two styles of bags,** one for week-long excursions and another for overnight trips."

in this book. I packed way too much crap and far too little important stuff. Too much is bad enough, but too little really sucks. Why? Because every year I forgot something, I ended up having to buy shit I already owned. I must have 20 beanies, ten pairs of clear glasses, a dozen bullshit sweatshirts, and a bunch of other miscellaneous riding shit that I'll never wear again but needed at the time just because I forgot to pack it. 🏍️

What to Pack

- ☠ Three to four T-shirts

- ☠ A pack of earplugs

- ☠ One or two beanies for cold nights (The combination of wearing a knit cap and ear plugs will save you from a major cold)

- ☠ Chaps

- ☠ Boots: Wear them so they don't take up any room

- ☠ A pair of sneakers (Chuck Taylors are my personal favorite)

- ☠ A hooded or fleece sweatshirt

- ☠ Three pairs of jeans plus what you're wearing

- ☠ A helmet that you can attach to the outside of your bag

- ☠ Five pairs of socks, can't have enough of these

- ☠ Clear glasses and regular sunglasses

- ☠ A disc lock. This is the smallest lock that provides pretty good security. It attaches to your disc brake; just don't forget to take it off before you start riding. I can't tell you how many guys I've seen fuck up their disc or fall because they forgot to take off the lock.

- ☠ Leather jacket; wear it if you can, it will take up less room

- ☠ Gloves

- Two button-down Dickies shirts, one long sleeve and one short sleeve

- Rain gear, including booties

- All of your personal hygiene shit, which I will leave to your discretion. However, worse-case scenario is that you buy what you forget at the local drug store when you get there.

- Seems like a short list, right? Well these are the essentials. Everything you can fit after that is gravy.

Chapter Five

DON'T BE "THAT GUY"...

You Know Exactly What I Mean!

OK. You've made it this far and if you learned anything about the American motorcycle culture you'll know that it can be summed up in two words: Discovery and authenticity. So that's why this chapter is named the way it is.

In every sport, hobby, or lifestyle, there's "that guy." You know, the jock at the football games who paints his face and takes off his shirt when it's ten below zero, or the overzealous hunter who carries his hunting rifle in the back of his pickup truck, just in case. Give me a break. You know the guys I'm talking about. In this culture there are plenty of those guys, so here's a little review of the most important things I talked about right at the beginning of the book:

☠ Do not wear giant logos or fringe on your jacket.

☠ Do not wear one of those pseudo-Nazi-style fake helmets.

☠ In general, try not to draw extra attention to yourself if you just bought your bike two weeks ago.

When you're on the road:

☠ Don't ride up alongside of or really close to a car and rev your engine constantly trying to act really cool.

☠ Don't zigzag in between cars like you're playing a video game.

☠ When you walk into a restaurant, don't talk extra loud and use bad language to make everyone think you're a big bad biker and they should be afraid of you. What they'll mostly be thinking is "What an asshole." This just plays into a ridiculous stereotype.

- ☠ If you see a biker in trouble on the side of the road, pull over and help. This is a big deal. There is a brotherhood when it comes to helping each other on the road. Don't fuck it up. You should also offer roadside assistance to any motor vehicle that is broken down. Bikers have a reputation for being helpful, so let's keep that alive. How many times have you heard someone say, "Then this big old biker pulled over and gave me a hand. Even though he was pretty scary looking, he was the nicest guy." The road is a major part of our culture. Help take care of it.

- ☠ Don't wear the leather jacket you ride in, covered in patches and pins, as your normal street jacket. When you are going to the corner store for a pack of smokes, it's not necessary for everyone to know you're a badass biker.

- ☠ Don't talk about yourself and your motorcycle experiences at every family function or with your friends who don't share the same passion. You don't have to constantly prove you're a biker.

- ☠ Don't be a biker because you think it will make you a more interesting person. I know plenty of boring bikers and wild accountants. When I hear a guy constantly talking about motorcycles and all of his motorcycle experiences outside the biker community, all I can think is that he's trying to convince himself that he's cool.

- ☠ Don't act like you know everything about being a biker. As I said, I know a few things on this subject, and thank God I keep my mouth shut half the time and listened to the guys around me.

- ☠ Don't drink and ride. Guys who are usually talking the most shit do it when they are drunk (actually, we all talk shit when we're drunk . . . including me). It's harmless. Getting on your bike drunk is not. I don't drink and get on a bike anymore, but I did for years. What changed my mind wasn't the fact that I could have really hurt, or even killed, someone or myself. It was economics. Darryl got arrested in Sturgis one year and it cost him $1,500 and a day in jail! It could have cost him $10,000 or more, if convicted of a DUI.

The Day I Smartened Up

Darryl had just got out of jail several hours earlier, but there we were again on our bikes, drunk. As I approached the town of Sturgis my bike kept stalling, so I had to reach down repeatedly and restart it. This happened several times over. Each time I reached down I would swerve from side to side, which made me look drunk . . . and I was.

Suddenly Darryl's whole jumpsuit-wearing experience sleeping on a rubber mat with 40 other hardcore criminals flashed before my eyes. Realizing that the bike *wasn't going to stay running* and I was going to get pulled over at any second for drunk driving, I pulled over on my own.

> "Suddenly Darryl's whole jumpsuit-wearing experience sleeping on a rubber mat with 40 other hardcore criminals flashed before my eyes."

At most rallies you can pull into a bar parking lot, tell them you're too drunk to ride, and they'll let you lock up your bike for the night. I pulled over in front of the Broken Spoke Saloon, limped my bike in, Darryl and Paul followed. I simply told the guy at the gate that I needed to lock our bikes up for the night because we were drinking. He said "no problem."

Unfortunately, getting a cab in Sturgis is a pain in the ass and takes forever. After 20 minutes of waiting, Darryl started busting my balls telling me that he was pretty sure we could ride home safely. We probably could have, but something that night just didn't

> "Pull into a bar parking lot, tell them you're too drunk to ride, and they'll let you lock up your bike for the night."

feel right. So I told him that I would pay for the cab and food and keep a running total of how much cash it cost. At the end of the ordeal I would deduct that sum from the $1,500 he spent getting out of jail and see who came out ahead. The cab and a few cheeseburgers cost me $45. I came out way ahead and we all slept in a nice comfortable hotel bed that night. I won that bet. From that day on I haven't been on a bike drunk.

When I plan to party, I take a cab and I'm pretty sure Darryl is also a convert. So if you don't have the common sense not to ride drunk for the obvious consequences, do it for the economic reasons. You can't lose.

BIKEOLOGY & TIP:
Support shirts

T-shirts clubs sell with their logo or an icon printed on it. Anyone can buy one. They do this to raise money, and it's fine to buy one—but **beware** where you are when you are wearing it.

The Top 10 Things to do and Not do When You Run into a Bunch of Motorcycle Club Members

Very early in this book I talked about different motorcycle clubs and how they've influenced the American motorcycle culture. I also defined the difference between a motorcycle club and a riding group. Simply put, the Hells Angels is a motorcycle club. The HOG, Harley Owners Group, is a riding organization. Never, ever, ever refer to a club as a "gang" or a club member as a "gang member." The Hells Angels literally call it the "G" word and there's no better way to piss them off than to use it in their presence. Same goes for other clubs and their members. Unless you enjoy eating your meals through tubes, I suggest eliminating the "G" word from your vocabulary.

A club member devotes his entire life and existence to the club. It's a lifelong commitment. Motorcycle clubs are like families. Fuck with one family member, you fuck with them all. They are tough, organized, and will do whatever it takes to protect their family. With that being said, follow these simple rules:

10. Don't walk up to a club member and have your buddy take a picture of you posing with him. Most club members do not like to have their pictures taken, and they don't like outsiders just walking up to them out of the blue.

9. Don't go around wearing club member logos or colors if you're not affiliated with the club. The Hell's Angels are known for two colors, red and white. Don't wear red and white and a support shirt thinking that makes you one of them. You'll probably just get your ass kicked by a rival club.

"Never, ever, ever refer to a club as a 'gang' or a club member as a 'gang member.'"

8. Don't walk up to a club member and start a conversation. If a club guy wants to talk to you, he will. Don't walk up and say shit like, "So how long you been in a biker gang, and how do I get in?" Not a good idea.

7. If you see a bike that belongs to a club member (you'll know by a sticker that usually says: Property of…) don't fuck with it or park really close to it. Park down the street. Again, being around them doesn't make you cool.

6. If you ride by their clubhouse, don't pull in thinking it's a local watering hole and belly up to the bar.

5. If you're in a bar and see a group of club members, don't send them a round of drinks and then walk over like you're the man. Save that pick-up technique for chicks. Club members have each other to drink with. Unless you're friends with one of them on a personal level, don't think buying a few drinks is going to get you accepted into their social scene.

4. When you're riding on the road and you come across a bunch of club members riding together, don't fall in with them like it's one for all, all for one. Clubs have their own rules on how they ride together and who they invite to ride with them. You can't just tag along.

3. Don't talk to people in bars and at rallies about your inside knowledge and how you think one club is better or cooler than the other. You know, shit like your friend is a Hells Angel, blah, blah, blah. Many clubs have their members hang around undercover without their colors on, checking out the scene. The reason for this is to see if rival club members are in their territory. If you start mouthing off about this club or that club, you might be considered a threat and get a good ass kicking. If you're not in a club, don't talk about it.

2. If you see a bunch of club members talking with a few girls, look the other way. If club guys are chatting with the ladies, you're out. The girls aren't fair game. The rule of every man for himself does not apply in this scenario.

1. And the number one thing to do when you find yourself around club members is *nothing*. Do not act differently. Do not be an asshole. Do not approach them. Just do nothing. If you find yourself in the middle of a bunch of club members and feel uncomfortable, just leave. There are plenty of places to hang out at rallies and bike events. If club members want to have the run of a bar, let them. Finish your drink and move along. If you think this makes you a pussy, get over it. There is absolutely no need to be a tough guy when it comes to encountering a motorcycle club. They will always win.

TIP:
Enjoying the open road is a lot easier when you know how to act.

Chapter Six

RALLY TIME

Laconia, Daytona, and Sturgis

There are three major motorcycle rallies, in my opinion, and several more that are growing. The majors are:

☠ Laconia Bike Week, New Hampshire

☠ Sturgis Bike Week, South Dakota

☠ Daytona Bike Week, Florida

I have been to all three several times so here are my opinions:

Laconia Bike Week
Date: Second week in June
Location: Laconia, New Hampshire

Laconia, New Hampshire, is the oldest bike rally. It started in 1923 with the Loudon Classic motorcycle race. This, like many other rallies, started and revolved around motorcycle races.

Laconia is my least favorite rally of the major three for two reasons. First, the weather. Every time I've been to Laconia, it's either 100 percent humidity or raining, as I mentioned before in my rain gear story. Also, the town is so small that there's really not that much to do once you're there.

The last time I went to Laconia was in 2004. I flew to New Jersey and met up with a bunch of friends I'd been riding with since 1992: Darryl, Ronnie, Mike, and a few new guys. One of the new cats had a GPS on his bike and declared himself the leader. Why I let this happen I don't know, but it was a bad idea. My family owned a house in New Hampshire and I practically grew up there. I knew how to get to Laconia, but I kept my mouth shut.

Normally the ride from North Jersey to Laconia is about four to five hours. I should have known after an hour when we were riding around in some state park in New York, this was going to be trouble. Thank you Mr. Fucking GPS! Four hours later we were in Massachusetts and everyone was pretty pissed off.

Having been up to Laconia before with the same group, we all knew that there was a great strip club in Massachusetts so, of course, we took a break and found the club. We vowed that we'd have one beer and we'd hit the road. Of course, when you've been riding in circles for five hours and you finally get a break in a very fun strip club, one beer ain't gonna happen.

Three hours later we left the club, too buzzed to ride, but with little choice. We had at least three more hours to go and the plan was to follow the guy with the GPS. However, at ten o'clock at night, "following the GPS guy" was out of the question. Five minutes out of the parking lot three guys went one way, two another, and two yet another. It was every man for himself. I, of course, was with Mike because we were the only two who rode close to the speed limit. The other guys were either 10 miles an hour too slow or 20 miles an hour too fast. Also, I was on Mike's Bad Boy and good judgment says to stay with the guy who is letting you borrow his bike.

About an hour later, Mike and I pulled into a tollbooth to get our bearings and, wouldn't ya know it, a State Highway Patrol car pulled in right behind me. I could have never passed a breathalyzer test, especially in Massachusetts, so I went on the offensive. I got off my bike and walked over to the cop car and asked directions to Laconia.

The cop was a giant black guy who could have played pro football, and when I asked him directions he just looked at me and laughed. My heart sank. I thought for sure I was toast. Instead he told me he was laughing at me because I was so far off course.

"Fortunately, he was pretty cool and gave me some quick directions to get back on track, and five f&#king hours later Mike and I were in Laconia."

Fortunately, he was pretty cool and gave me some quick directions to get back on track, and five fucking hours later Mike and I were in Laconia. The rest of the group pulled in shortly after.

It was 2 a.m. by then, and the normally six-hour road trip had taken 14 hours. Did I mention that this was my first time shooting for *American Thunder* and I was meeting my camera guy there?

At 2 a.m. I assumed the camera guy would be passed out and we would regroup in the morning to start shooting. But no, there he was, wide awake, standing in the door. Now, just to set the scene a little better, my father had passed away just a few days earlier so all I could think was that something else in my family went terribly wrong. As I walked into the house, beat up from the feet up, the cameraman walked over to me and gave me some shitty news. The $40,000 camera had been smashed on the plane. This was not something I wanted to hear at 2 a.m., especially after the ride from Hell.

Luckily, the next morning, my local production assistant was able to rent a camera from a local news station and with a little jury-rigging we were cool. However, this was the last time I would ever use this camera operator to shoot for *American Thunder*.

The trip was pretty uneventful except for dosing one of our friends with a few Valiums so we could steal a shirt from him. Even that didn't work, and the bastard still got the shirt back at the end of the trip.

By the third day we had all had enough and started home. We were all exhausted and the ride home did not sound like fun.

On the way home the guys took off and left me in the dirt. Mike had left a day earlier so I was on my own. I was so tired that I lay on my tank and just cracked the throttle averaging 85 miles per hour, not typical for me. Just as I crossed into Massachusetts, the first thing I saw was a green Mustang lit up and coming after me. It was an undercover state patrol car.

The cop pulls me over, comes over to my bike, and because I was so wiped out I say in total defeat, "You got me." The cop looks at me and smiles, "Don't remember me, do ya." I looked a little harder at him and suddenly realized it was the same giant ex-football player cop who had given me directions three days ago at the toll station.

"Going to a rally like Daytona or Sturgis is not a typical trip. Shit will happen, and how you deal with it will change the way you look at the American motorcycle culture and the people who live it forever."

He must have seen the shape I was in and felt sorry for me because he let me go. Ten miles down the road I noticed that he had pulled over another group of guys. Yep, it was my speed demon friends. Perfect! I think he let them go, too. Anyway, that's about the most fun (if you can call it that) that I ever had going to Laconia.

Don't get me wrong, if you live within a few hundred miles of this rally, you should definitely go, but I don't recommend traveling across country for it.

Daytona Bike Week
Date: First week of March
Location: Daytona Beach, Florida

Daytona Bike Week could be an entire book on its own. In 1992 I convinced several guys I had known for only a year or two that we should make this trip together. Because there were seven of us, I thought that the best thing to do was to rent a house rather than find several hotel rooms or camp.

Going to a rally like Daytona or Sturgis is not a typical trip. Shit will happen, and how you deal with it will change the way you look at the American motorcycle culture and the people who live it forever.

Not only was this my first major rally, but I was also getting my 1987 Harley Heritage delivered. This was the one that I put everything on, including the kitchen sink. My partner in Old Mission Scooters, a small bike shop in Traverse City, Michigan, John Villanueva, was putting the finishing touches on the bike and was going to haul it for me to Connecticut.

Once there, the plan was to head south to New Jersey, hook up with the other guys, load our bikes on the Ryder truck, and get on the road to Daytona.

These aren't the original seven from Daytona 1992, but this is the main group of guys who have taken most of our trips together.

Right to left: Eddie, Mark, Scotty, Me, Mike, Darryl, and Ronnie.

For several weeks, all of us planned who would do what for the big trip. Ray had a gas station and hooked up with Ryder, so he got us the truck cheap. Mike owned a company that manufactured installments for malls across the country so he built a subfloor with eyehooks and slots to accommodate the motorcycles. If it sounds like a lot of work, it was.

Getting back to the delivery of my bike from Michigan. John had fallen behind on the build and was still putting on shit the day he was supposed to leave. As you'll find out, building a bike is like building a house. It takes twice as much money and time as you originally plan. Anyway, John got the bike done the day before the truck was going to leave New Jersey, so now he had to drive for 24 hours straight to meet me in Connecticut. I was so stressed out that I couldn't sleep. At 7 a.m. on Friday morning, John pulled into my parents' driveway with my freshly built, freshly painted Heritage and his 1950 Panhead in the back of an old beat-up milk truck. I still can't believe the truck made the trip.

Now I had to get to New Jersey by noon so we could all leave. No problem, right? Wrong. I totally forgot that I had to register the bike. So pumped on stress and adrenaline, we ran the truck down to the DMV in lovely Bridgeport, Connecticut. To add insult to injury, it was 30 degrees outside.

We unloaded the bike and got in line for inspection. The inspector came over and started the inspection process, tick tock, tick tock. I was a mess, as you can guess, because the bike was so new that several things weren't really working

"John had fallen behind on the build and was still putting on shit the day he was supposed to leave."

very well. The worst of it was when the back caliper locked up, making it almost impossible to roll. The inspector sensed I was freaking and told me to come back another day when I had gotten all of the bugs worked out to finish the inspection.

I lost it. What could I do? Beg, that's what I could do. So I laid it on thick about it being a show bike, and I had to get to Daytona, etc. He actually went for it. Maybe because he saw John covered in grease assuring him that we would get the bike in tiptop

"By some small miracle, I passed the inspection and got my registration."

shape once we got to Florida. By some small miracle, I passed the inspection and got my registration, but now it was about 11:30 a.m. Remember, we were supposed to be leaving New Jersey at noon and five guys were standing around with a truck all loaded up waiting.

Cutting to the chase, we arrived in Jersey late, loaded our last two bikes, and hit the road. Now the plan was for two guys to drive in the Ryder and the rest to ride in the SUV. During the trip we'd take turns driving.

Right and Wrong

Here's a little quiz to see if you've been paying attention up until this point. What's wrong or right with this picture so far?

Here's what's right:

☠ We rented a house in Daytona.

Here's what's wrong:

☠ Seven guys who don't really know each other were going on a bike trip together.

☠ We were driving.

☠ I had a brand-new bike I had never ridden before, and it still needed work.

☠ All the guys from New Jersey were so excited about going to Daytona that they partied all night and were hungover.

☠ I hadn't slept and John had been driving from Michigan for a day straight.

☠ We were trusting more than $250,000 worth of motorcycles in the back of a truck to a bunch of really tired guys.

If this is your plan for an upcoming trip, stop right now!

Finally, we got on the road and divided up the driving. Who would sleep and who would drive, and when? Sounds logical, but it's not because we are all jacked up about the trip and everyone wanted to talk about the upcoming week of debauchery. So we all stayed awake for about five hours and then we all hit the wall. No one wanted to drive the SUV because it smelled like five guys, and no one wanted to drive the truck because no one wanted to be responsible for a damaged bike. It was pretty much a disaster.

"Within 15 minutes we were getting pulled over."

The new plan was to stop every few hours and load up on coffee, and that was the beginning of my problem. I won't bore you with the next 20 hours of driving, but I will tell you that between the seven of us we probably drank 10 gallons of fucking coffee.

Of course, nothing mattered when we finally pulled over the bridge and saw the sign that said "Welcome To Daytona Beach." Within 20 minutes we found our rental house. It was on A1A and backed up onto the beach. While the rest of the gang unloaded the bikes, went to the liquor store, and set up the house with supplies, I spent two hours taking off my back wheel to unlock the caliper and bleed my brake—not so fun.

The evening rolled around and we dressed up in our baddest of badass biker clothes. (Back then this included spurs on our boots. For some weird reason these were popular in the early 1990s.) Seven of us tore out of the driveway to Main Street, which was less than two miles down the strip. The guys wearing the spurs thought it would be cool to drag them on the ground shooting up sparks about 30 yards behind the bikes. It looked pretty cool, but the cops didn't think so. Within 15 minutes we were getting pulled over.

The cops were cool and let us off with a warning.

One thing everyone has to do at least once at Bike Week is actually ride up and down Main Street. It's like being in a *Mad Max* movie. There are thousands of bikes lined up on each side of the street, people are yelling and checking out the scene, the sidewalks and bars are packed.

TIP:

There are some pretty cool bike shows. The best is the Rat's Hole show. But if you can't make it, don't worry. Everything you'll want to see ends up on Main Street at some point. My best advice is to plan as little as possible; just do whatever you feel like doing. I hate the guys who have a fucking agenda for every day. It's Bike Week, not the Griswold family vacation.

As we drove down this gauntlet of bikes and bikers, we thought it would be cool if we started revving our bikes, some of which were loud because a few guys had straight pipes without baffles. Of course the crowds on the sidewalks went wild and started to cheer us on, so the louder they cheered the louder the seven of us revved. And so it went: cheering, revving, cheering, revving. What we didn't know was that you couldn't do this, and that's when the cops pulled us over for the second time.

We had literally been on our bikes in Daytona for less than an hour and we had been pulled over by the police twice. Again, the cops were cool and only issued us $35 tickets for wearing non-DOT-approved helmets.

That was the first day of my first bike trip. I can't remember exactly what happened for the rest of that night except that we all made it back to the house in one piece. We were pulled over by the cops twice. A fine start to the trip on all accounts.

Over the years that we've attended Daytona, we always rent that same house. We threw parties every night, played pool and Ping-Pong until dawn, and sat in the garage smoking and drinking until the sun came up. It was absolute heaven. I have never laughed so hard as I did on some of those nights. And even with all of the fuck-ups and the mistakes I've made over the years, I wouldn't trade those experiences for anything. These memories are exactly what the American motorcycle culture is all about.

"And even with all of the f&#k-ups and the mistakes I've made over the years, I wouldn't trade those experiences for anything. These memories are exactly what the American motorcycle culture is all about."

The second year the group went to Daytona, five of us flew and two guys drove the rental truck with the bikes. For that we gave them a break on their share of the rent for the house.

The third year was the last year we ever hauled our bikes in a rented truck. Since then we've had them shipped and everyone flies. I think the straw that broke the camel's back was that the two guys who said they would drive didn't really get along.

Stories of Daytona

Now, it would be impossible for me to tell you everything that has happened in Daytona all of the years I've attended, so I thought it might be cool to share some stories that stand out in my mind. I can't separate the years in which they happened, but they are all true.

Drunk tow truck ride

There's no pride in riding drunk, and people can get hurt. However, there was a time several years ago when we all threw caution to the wind, either for lack of maturity or brains, and got pretty tore up before riding.

On this one day in particular, we started drinking at 10a.m. and continued until about 7 or 8p.m. Somehow, all but one of us made it back to the house safely. The guy missing was Mike, the most responsible guy of the group. Nobody knew quite what to do. I mean you can't call the police and file a missing person's report. No one knew the area well enough to start searching aimlessly. So we decided to wait.

A few hours later we were all sitting in the garage still wondering what to do. Was he hurt, or something worse?

About 10 minutes into our worst-case scenarios, here came Mike pulling up in a cop car. He jumped out of the car and started yelling, "Get my camera, get my camera." He blew by us into the house and came back in 30 seconds with his camera. We thought he

was in some kind of trouble and wanted to photograph the cops, but the cops took off and now we were even more confused.

Then, almost on cue, a tow truck pulled into our driveway carrying Mike's brand-new Softail Heritage in a cradle suspended on the hook—a bizarre sight. Mike wanted the camera to get a picture of it before the guy actually lowered the bike and took off.

It seems that night before Mike forgot where he parked his bike. While he was looking for it, he passed out in some bushes in front of a hotel. A cop found him and woke him up. At that point Mike saw that the bike was just a few yards from where he passed out. Realizing that he couldn't drive home, the cop was nice enough to call a tow truck and offer Mike a ride. Yes, believe it or not, this cop was so cool that he actually wanted to be helpful instead of just busting balls.

The tow truck came, hoisted up the bike, and Mike got into the car. Then the cop asked him where he was staying. That was a problem. Mike forgot the address, so the cop drove up and down A1A until Mike recognized the house. Mike didn't even get a ticket.

90 Miles Per Hour on A1A

There's always one guy in the crew who attracts trouble, whether he wants to or not. It's just in his nature. That guy in our group is Darryl. Darryl is the kind of guy who, despite

BIKEOLOGY:
A1A

The state road that runs along the Florida coast through Daytona Beach from Key West to Callahan, just south of Georgia.

his laid-back "live and let live" attitude, gets into more trouble with the law than anyone I know, even if he's not doing anything wrong.

This time, however, he was doing something wrong, and that something was seeing how fast his bike could go down A1A. He probably got it up to 90 miles per hour, about 50 miles per hour over the speed limit. Of course, this caught the attention of a motorcycle cop who promptly pulled him over.

Besides getting into trouble, Darryl also has the gift of gab, especially when it comes to police.

Pretty pissed off, the cop said, "Hey man, you know you were going almost 100 miles per hour!?"

Darryl, in the way only he can, replied, "Hey, that's really great. You want to give it a try while I'll hang here on your bike?"

Then he began literally to get on the cop's bike. Completely caught off guard, the cop just bursts out laughing. All I could figure is that the cop was so flabbergasted that he just couldn't think of anything to say except "OK. That's enough. Take a hike, slow down, and have a nice week."

Fatboy on Stage

The Pink Pony was the first strip club the guys and I found in Daytona. There are others right in town such as the Shark Lounge, Molly Brown's, and the latest greatest Lollipops. But for some reason the Pink Pony was the first one that caught our eye.

Over the past dozen or so years Florida has changed. There are strip club laws ranging from "anything goes" to the girls having to wear pasties over their nipples. Why? Who the fuck knows? Thankfully things are pretty cool again. The girls get naked, you can smoke and drink, hurray! This particular story happened in the early 1990s when the rules were pretty much "anything goes."

On this particular night Ray, a guitar-playing rock-and-roll party animal, who stood about 5 feet 7 inches tall, had jet black hair down to his belt, and looked like a complete wild man, was part of our group.

Ray had a 1990 Fatboy, one of the first ones made with a gray paint job and yellow striped rocker boxes. The only custom change Ray made to the bike was

"Thankfully things are pretty cool again. The girls get naked, you can smoke and drink, hurray!"

to change the exhaust. However, he didn't bother to re-jet the carb or tune the bike to match the new pipes, which happened to be 2-inch open straight pipes.

Imagine how a stock Harley would run with 2-inch straight pipes. Can't picture it? Then let me try to describe it: ear splitting, back firing, and 3-foot flames shooting out the ends. Pretty dramatic.

One night as we all partied at the Pony, the owner came around and got pretty friendly with Ray. As they were talking, the owner mentioned that he thought it would be cool

if some guy would just ride through the doors, drive up on to the stage, and rev the shit out of his bike. I'm not quite sure if what happened next was actually planned, but suddenly the doors flew open, we all heard a bike revving the throttle to the max, then boom!! Ray and his Fatboy came racing into the club, up a ramp, and right onto the stage.

I couldn't believe it was happening! Ray with his rock star long black hair was revving his bike, smoke was filling the club, the noise was awesome, and flames were shooting out of the tail pipes. The people in the club were on their feet, the DJ pumped up the music, the girls started dancing naked around the bike and grinding on Ray. You couldn't get a better show at an Ozzy concert.

To this day I have never seen something so over-the-top and spontaneous in a strip club. Also, I was never happier for a crazy friend who, for five minutes in Daytona at the Pink Pony, got to live out a crazy fantasy.

A Wire that Cost $400

Remember when I said you should never bring a brand-new bike, or at least a bike you just worked on, to a rally? Well here's just one reason why.

For many of the years that I went to Daytona I brought my 1987 Heritage. Yes, the one with so much shit on it that if I sold everything on eBay I would have had enough money to buy another whole bike. Regardless, this was my bike, my baby, and during the winter months when I couldn't ride it I was adding shit to it.

Because I lived on the East Coast at the time, Daytona bike week marked the beginning of the riding season for me. This meant that after fooling with my bike all winter, Daytona was the test ground to see how everything would work. Bad idea. This particular year I was on a bullet-light kick. Bullet lights are small, old-school torpedo-shaped lights. I really wanted the bike to have that cool 1950s look with lights on the fender rails, around the license plate, and for good measure I thought it would be cool to hide a few behind the carb so the motor would light up at night.

Since then, of course, they make several products that are actually designed to do just that, the Küryakyn Lizard light being one of them. Back then you had to fabricate custom mounts and run wires all over the place to get it to work. So over the course of the winter, with too much time on my hands, I hooked up at least a dozen lights and, wanting perfection, hid all of the wires under the seat and anywhere out of sight where I could fit them.

"What the f&#k is a module?"

Bike Week finally rolled around and I went to Daytona with the guys and, as usual, we hit it hard right away. As soon as I got down the road, I noticed my bike was constantly cutting out. Pissed off, I limped it back to the garage to try and see what the problem was.

One of the guys told me that this kind of shit happens all of the time when you wire additional lights on your bike and that the module, located under the seat, could have been fried. When I heard this, my response was "What the fuck is a module?" So my buddy explained to me that the module is a small computer that acts as the brains for your

BIKEOLOGY:
Limp it back

Gently riding your bike in first or second gear just to get it to a place you can fix it.

bike and all the electrical connections plug into it. That's not quite accurate, but in Daytona, at Bike Week, with a dead motorcycle on my hands, it sounded right.

Basically, all I wanted to do was fix it and get back to the fun as soon as possible. I believed what my pal was telling me, so I set out to find a new module. In Daytona, back then, there was only one real place to get motorcycle parts and that was Miller's. Also back then, unlike today, there were a lot of unreliable bikes on the road, spillovers from the AMF days. Today

"It was either spend the money or don't ride, so I spent the money."

you can go to J&P Cycles and get whatever you need fast. Also, Harleys don't break down very much these days so everything's a lot easier.

Miller's, however, was the place that year. So I trekked out there and waited in line for two hours. When I got to the front of the line, I asked the service guy for a module and he told me that for electrical parts I need to be in another line, so I waited another 30 minutes in that line. Meanwhile, all of my buddies were out having the time of their lives.

I finally got what I thought was the right part, and a few other things that I was told I needed for installing the module, and the total came to . . . $400! Now I'm just plain pissed off. This module was a plastic box about a half-inch thick, 4 inches wide, and 6 inches long. And $400 was about half of the spending money I had for the entire week. What the fuck! It was either spend the money or don't ride, so I spent the money.

I got back to the house and my friend, the one who told me that I needed the module in the first place, told me to start taking off the seat, unhook the battery, pull the starter motor, etc. Basically there was a whole lot of shit to take off because this module was located under the battery box and behind the starter, not a real convenient spot. Estimated time to do the job: four fucking hours, according to the manual that he just happened to have with him.

Now I'm steaming. My day is shot. I'm sweating in the garage, it's 4:00 p.m., and the rest of the guys just got back from a great day of partying and riding. Obviously, they all see that I'm in no mood to fuck around so they all kind of slinked by me into the house where I can hear them laughing their asses off. I had to suck it up and get the job done or I'd be there all night.

I got about halfway into tearing everything apart and as I was about to pull the starter I noticed that one small black wire under the seat was broken. To this day I don't know exactly what the wire was for. However, I was pretty sure it got pinched when I wired all of those goddamn bullet lights, but I didn't disccover this until I rode the bike in Daytona.

Desperate to end this fiasco, and going on a hunch, I reconnected the wire, bolted all of the old shit back in place at record speed, and guess what? I hit the starter button and the bike roared to life.

I just fixed the wire and was pretty happy to be rolling out for the night on two wheels.

All sales final

OK. So even though I wasted all day and spent $400, the bike was running. I figured I'd return the parts in the morning. I headed out with the boys and partied hard. I was happy that my bike was running again. I dropped some coin celebrating. The next morning I rode back out to Miller's, stood in line (this time for only an hour because it was the return line), got to the counter, smiled, handed the parts back in their original unopened blister packs, and asked ever so nicely for my $400 back. The sales guy smiled back, looked at me, and pointed to a sign that said "ALL SALES FOR ELECTRONICS ARE FINAL."

"You can't return electric parts or at least back then you couldn't. Maybe now you can, but ask first before you buy them."

For years that goddamn module sat in my garage reminding me of a hard and expensive lesson. You can't return electric parts, or at least back then you couldn't. Maybe now you can, but ask first before you buy them.

Not Funny!

Of course, for several years to follow this became the running joke between all of the guys. One year they pulled my spark plug wires off just enough so the bike misfired while I was riding it. They had a pretty big laugh when we pulled over and I started freaking out saying that I must have broken another wire, and I was sick of this shit…blah, blah, blah.

One year the joke was as simple as turning off my gas so the bike started to sputter and cut out as we rode back to the house.

Another year they poured oil under my bike to make it look like a leak. However, I was getting wise to their bullshit by then and I called them on it. They swore it wasn't a joke and that I should take a closer look. Sure as shit, drops of oil were coming off the bottom of the primary. To make the joke look totally believable, they had rubbed some oil on the primary and then had poured a little on the ground under the bike so it appeared to be an active leak. I, of course, went into a tirade, and they, of course, busted out laughing. By the way, if any of you guys are reading this, I haven't forgotten, so beware.

BIKEOLOGY:
Road rash

This is when you hit the pavement or black top and a few layers of skin get ground up. It's superficial but painful.

You can't keep a good man down

Although my story about breaking down and getting fucked for $400 worth of parts is pretty good, it really can't compare with the one year Darryl completely wiped out.

Darryl had a 1990-something Fatboy, and he had just got done customizing it back in New Jersey. This was going to be its debut journey to Daytona. Besides the custom wheels and chrome, Darryl had painted the bike purple and cream. We affectionately referred to it as the Easter egg. The bike was gorgeous by the standards of the day. D-man also replaced the handlebars with some short drag bars, which looked great but threw off the geometry, which he didn't know at the time.

It's not uncommon for Darryl to have a girl on the back of a bike every now and then. On this particular day, we had all just come back to the house to get ready for the evening's festivities when we noticed Darryl missing. Like good friends, we argued over who was going to find him. I think it was Ronnie who ended up having to go. Five minutes later Ronnie was back. I was a little confused and asked, "Where's Darryl?"

Ronnie's response was "He was right behind me." Before we could really ask Ronnie any more questions, we saw Darryl limping his bike up the driveway, all fucked up, but with a very attractive young lady on the back.

It seems that the "too short" drag bars made it very difficult for him to make tight turns, especially with a passenger on the back. So while he was making a corner, he hit some sand, overcorrected, and boom, down they went.

Now, the first thing we all wanted to know was if anyone was hurt, and the answer was "not really" except for some nasty road rash.

I thought, as everyone else did, that this 20-something college co-ed would be throwing a fit, or at least wanting a ride home as fast as possible, but that wasn't the case. Even bruised, bleeding, and a little busted up, Darryl convinced his date to come inside and clean up. Five of us stood in the garage pretty much in shock while he escorted this very

Not looking so good.

understanding and attractive young lady into his bedroom.

It was obvious that she wasn't leaving, he wasn't going to the hospital, and that his bike was going to be out of commission for the week. What were we going to do?

Scotty works his magic

On this particular year, we happened to have Scotty with us. Scotty was a certified Harley mechanic and stereotypical biker. He stands 6 feet 3 inches, weighs around 300 pounds, and sports a big old beard. Scotty had thrown a whole mess of tools in the truck. He immediately grabbed them and went to work.

The worst of the damage was the tank, which was pretty much a complete bust. The rest of the damage was

Most of the bike disassembled.

cosmetic. With a trip to the parts store and some hard work, it appeared everything could be salvaged.

None of us wanted Darryl to be without a bike all week, so with Scotty at the lead we all pitched in. A few of us took off to wrangle parts while the others tore all of the damaged components off the bike. As a team, we all worked into the night and were able to get most everything back on the bike except the right half of the tank.

Interestingly enough, the young lady who was with Darryl spent the night. It was pretty entertaining for the rest of us because all night we kept hearing her yell, "Ouch, oh shit, ouch that hurts," and then "yes, yes, yes, oh yeah."

That morning everything seemed fine except for half of the gas tank. It was painted with matte brown primer, so the bike wouldn't look great but it would run fine.

Scotty assesses the damage as Mark looks on.

Having just finished the custom paint job a few weeks earlier, and wanting to have a killer ride during Bike Week, the primer-painted tank was totally unacceptable to Darryl. I explained to him that the color was a custom mix and he was just going to have to ride the bike like it was for the week and be happy. Things could be a lot worse.

Darryl's plan

Darryl had his own plan. He grabbed the primed tank and he and Ronnie hopped into our rental car and took off. The rest of us ate breakfast and carried on with the day. After riding a little we all headed back to the house to see if Darryl and Ronnie were back from wherever they went. I assumed they were just going to take the hot co-ed home and grab a bite to eat. Fifteen minutes after we pulled in, they followed.

Here's what they did: They found an auto body shop and told the owner that they would give him a $100 tip on top of whatever it cost to paint the tank in a few hours.

Darryl riding the perfectly repaired Fatboy on the beach— back when you could ride on the beach.

BIKEOLOGY:
Split Tank

Many Harley- or American-made gas tanks come in two sections, a right and left half.

The guy agreed. Then they dropped the chick off. At that point, Darryl realized that his arm wasn't quite right so Ronnie took him to the hospital. There he was told that he had a cracked collarbone. The doctor gave him some painkillers, a sling, and sent him on his way. That took about four hours. On the way back from the hospital, they stopped at the auto body shop and, guess what? The tank was finished and was painted perfectly new.

Once back at the house, Scotty bolted the tank back on, hooked up the gas line, and I swear you would have never known that the bike had been in a wreck the day before.

Darryl showered, changed, put his arm in the sling, took a few pain pills, and came out to the garage. We propped his arm up on the throttle, jumped on our bikes, and off we went.

The entire ordeal from start to finish took 22 hours, and we never missed a beat. Hell, yeah!

The Little Mermaid

When I was a kid I was an all-state swimmer. A 5 a.m. swim wasn't a big deal back then, but 10 years later in March at Bike Week it certainly took on a whole new meaning. During Bike Week, one of the things I was, and I repeat "was," notorious for was partying on the last night. My reason was simple: I could sleep on the plane on the way home. This particular year was no exception.

It was Saturday night and we had to catch a plane at 9 a.m. the next morning out of Daytona Beach International Airport. Not a big deal. With that in mind, and being my

WHO SAID THERE'S NO SUCH THING AS MERMAIDS?

over indulgent self, I announced that I was going out. I have no idea where I went, but I got pretty hammered—actually, really hammered.

I rolled back to the house at about 4:30 a.m. and, what do ya know, all the boys were sitting in the garage hanging out. They were packed and ready to leave in a few hours, but they also wanted to get in the last few hours of hanging out before heading home. I needed to take a piss, so I headed into the house, passed through the pool area, and saw a girl swimming naked in the pool. At least that's how I remember it. I was drunk, the underwater pool lights were casting some crazy shadows, and the whole thing was a freaky little trip. So much so that all I could think was: "Wow, there's a mermaid in the pool."

I stood there for about five minutes just watching this girl swim all around the pool. I was in a trance—a drug-induced alcoholic trance—but nevertheless, it was peaceful.

Then suddenly I hear, "Hey, Barbieri, if you like the pool so much why don't you take a swim?" Before I had time to react, one of my pals, rammed me from the back and CRASH—I was in the pool. Because it was a cold night, I had on my leather jacket, sweatshirt, and chaps, so when I hit the water I immediately sunk 9 feet straight to the bottom. But as I sunk, I was kind of in this euphoric state.

Underwater visions

Suddenly everything was dead quiet and the little mermaid was still swimming back and forth. I really couldn't see shit, but my mind saw it all as clear as day. Time stood still. When I hit the bottom I just kind of sat there staring. I have no idea how much time passed, but I don't remember freaking out trying to catch my breath. However, I probably should have.

The next thing I remember was that I was on my back, out of the pool, with three guys standing around me.

I weigh about 220 pounds dry. With wet leather, I've got to be close to three bills. I have no idea how they fished me out, but they did. No one was laughing. It was dead quiet and Mark gave me an "are you out of your mind?" look and asked why I just sat there on the bottom of the pool. I believe I muttered something about a naked chick looking like a mermaid. To this day I'm not even 100 percent sure that there even was a girl in the pool. If there was, she was gone by the time I got pulled out. Now it was 6 a.m. and I had only two hours to pack and get to the airport. No problem!

Suddenly I was motivated and got my shit together. I grabbed an empty plastic trash bag, shoved my wet clothes inside, and wrapped it all in a towel. Then I packed the rest of my shit into my T-Bag. I laid down for what seemed like two minutes and then joined the rest of the group in the garage to wait for Randy (the guy who hauled our bikes that year) to pick up the bikes.

"Despite all of the bullshit, we made it to the airport, but we had another problem— what do we do with our bikes?"

Now Randy was supposed to come by the house and drive us to the airport. We would give him our keys, and he would go back to the house and load the bikes into his truck to be hauled back to New Jersey. Ten minutes went by, then 20, and no Randy. Oh shit! Just then we realized that it was the last day of Bike Week and the parade had started.

The bike parade

The bike parade happens every year on the last Sunday of Daytona Bike Week, and thousands of bikes participate. That means that all of the streets are blocked off with cops and roadblocks, no traffic gets in or out, and that meant no Randy. This left us with only one choice: ride our bikes to the airport. We strapped as much luggage as possible to our bikes with rope and bungee cords.

We hopped on the bikes and then the fun really started. Somehow we had to cut through and cut off parade traffic. This little game was pretty nasty. We pissed off hundreds of bikers, sped through lights, stop signs, and pretty much broke every law in the book. During this complete disaster, I was still drunk and had not slept in more than 24 hours. Despite all of the bullshit, we made it to the airport, but we had another problem—what do we do with our bikes?

By some insane chance of fate, Randy pulled into the airport parking lot for some completely unrelated errand he had to do for another customer. We flagged him down, gave him our keys, and just like that the whole thing worked itself out.

I was still feeling pretty hungover and beat up, and I must have been bitching like a little girl because one of my buddies gave me a Percocet so I would shut up and pass out on the plane. Then my luck turned around. I managed to upgrade my seat to first class. I was starting to feel good from the painkiller.

There I was, in first class, chilling out. The Percocet was doing its job, and life was good. Then this very lovely stewardess started to serve drinks and put her cart right in front of my seat blocking me in, and that's when the booze, the 5 a.m. near-drowning, the mad dash to the airport, and the

"With only one option left, I grabbed the barf bag in the seat pocket and puked my guts out."

recently ingested painkiller hit me like a ton of bricks. Trying to keep my shit together, I very politely asked the stewardess if she would kindly move her cart so I could use the bathroom. She said "No." So I asked again, not so politely, and again she said "No."

I was in a panic. I had to get out of my seat because I was definitely going to be sick. With only one option left, I grabbed the barf bag in the seat pocket and puked my guts out.

I have to give credit to the engineers who designed these bags, because I filled it exactly to the top and didn't spill a drop, thank you God. I then folded over the top and clamped the little metal bendable tabs over the sides to secure it. "Miss Lovely," the stewardess, was too busy pouring drinks to see all this happen, so I politely got her attention and handed her the puke-filled bag and passed out. The next thing I remembered was waking up in Newark as we touched down. The perfect end to Bike Week!

Holy Hell

There is a town just outside of Daytona, literally right across the city line, named Holly Hill. One night the guys and I went to the Pink Pony. Yes, the same Pink Pony where Ray rode his bike on stage. We were leaving the place and yes, we were pretty drunk. Again, just let me say that I never drink and ride anymore and I advise strongly against it.

The five of us hopped on our bikes and started to head back to the house. There are only three turns you have to make to get back to the house. It's only a 5- or 6-mile ride and you're home free. So the chance of us getting in trouble in Holly Hill was pretty slim; the cops only have a two-minute window to nab you. Now, as I said before, I never ride fast but this one time I just felt like cracking the throttle, so *bang* I took off. The rest of the crew being speed freaks couldn't handle that I was out in front, so they cracked it and flew by me. I was doing at least 70 miles per hour in a 40 miles per hour zone, so they had to go past me at 100 miles per hour.

TIP:

The best thing you can do if your friends get pulled over is drive by, wait down the road, and assess the scene out of sight from the cops. Do not pull over with them right away. Chances are you'll get in trouble too.

Within seconds, two SUVs had the street in front of us blocked and several cops with white cowboys hats (I shit you not) are flagging us down with guns drawn. I had just enough time to react, slow down, and drive by but the guys in front of me got pulled over.

Darryl gets busted

About a mile up the street everyone who didn't get pulled over decided to go back to try to help the guys who did get pulled over. From our previous encounters with the law (and there have been many), we figured that it would be a slap on the wrist and everyone would be let go.

As we drove back, I saw Bobby sitting in the back of the police SUV, handcuffed, with his helmet still on his head. Not a good sign. So we pulled over and attempted to approach the cops to see if we could get a handle on the situation. The first guy in the group to speak was Darryl who says, "So, what's up?" And before he can get another word out, the 357-magnum-toting cowboy cop got in his face and yelled, "Hey boy, you want to go to jail, too?"

Bewildered, Darryl responded, "Me?" And that's all it took. The cop yanked him off his bike, slammed him against the car, cuffed him, and threw him in the back of the other SUV.

The rest of us were freaked out and eased off down the road again. This shit was getting heavy. All we could think was, "What the fuck just happened?" It looked like our friends just robbed a bank and were on the FBI's top 10 most wanted list.

It was a ridiculous scene. The street was blocked off. Lights were flashing. Cops were pacing, and our guys were handcuffed in the back of two SUVs with their helmets still on.

One of the guys in the group, Eddie, a New Jersey firefighter, said that he would ride back again and this time flash his badge and see if the boys in blue would take it easy. Eddie was back in five minutes. He told us that as he showed his badge the cops asked if he wanted to go to jail, too. Then the tow truck showed up.

There we were. It was 2:30 in the morning, there were five guys and seven bikes parked on the side of the road, two of our friends were on their way to jail, and the tow truck driver looked like once he took the bikes we would never see them again. Oh, yeah, and we were all drunk.

"It's always a bad sign when cops pull you over wearing cowboy hats, especially when it is not an official part of their uniform."

Thinking fast, Ronnie grabbed a few $20 bills and bribed the tow truck driver not to take the two bikes. The guy went for it and we stashed Darryl's and Bobby's bikes in the bushes. Eddie and one other guy drove to the police station to find out about bail. When Eddie returned we were still waiting on the side of the road smoking and bullshitting.

He told us that he flashed his badge at the police station and this time it helped a little. Darryl and Bobby were in a holding cell, handcuffed, with their helmets on and they were going to be charged with reckless driving. However, because Eddie was a fire-fighter the cops were going to release them in an hour and we could pick them up on the back steps of the jailhouse. No shit! Really! On the back steps of the jail, not in the front lobby, no papers to sign, just pick them up around back in an hour.

An hour later and sure as shit there they were sitting on the back steps of the jail-house just like the cops promised. I think Bobby still had his helmet on. We pulled their bikes out of the woods and the seven of us rode back to the house. It was around 5:00 or 6:00 in the morning.

Just as we were leaving the Holly Hill city limits, I looked in my rearview mirror and a cop was pulling me over. Un-fucking believable! The rest of the guys were way in front of me, so I'm pretty much thinking I'm screwed. Then I see that it's a Daytona cop this time, so at least I'm not in Holly Hill. And this cop doesn't have a cowboy hat on. (It's always a bad sign when cops pull you over wearing cowboy hats, especially when it is not an official part of their uniform.)

The cop comes up to me and, desperate not to go through what Darryl and Bobby have just experienced, I launch into the whole story of a few hours ago. I'm going through every detail, really laying it on, trying to sound pathetic and probably doing a good job of it. Finally, the cop, tired of my rambling, stops me and says, "Relax kid, I'm just giving you a warning about not coming to a complete stop at the stop sign. In Holly Hill they hate bikers and Bike Week. You see, they don't make very much money from the event like Daytona does so they love to bust you guys and hit you up with big fines. We call it Holy Hell during Bike Week."

Then he hands me my warning, tells me to have a nice day, and leaves. Holy Hell is right! I believe it cost Darryl a few grand between the fines and the lawyers to get him out of that one.

Drown the Clown

One of my favorite places to hang out during Bike Week in Daytona is the Iron Horse Saloon. It's loud, dirty, crowded, and it has several bars, good music, and great food–everything essential for the perfect biker bar.

One day, the usual suspects and I were there for maybe five or six hours and it was starting to get dark. So we decided to take one more lap around and then hit the road. On the way out we came across, believe it or not, a dunk tank. You know, the ones you see at carnivals. Some poor soul sits on a bench suspended over a tank of water while people throw baseballs at a little target in hopes of releasing the bench and knocking the person into the water.

The Iron Horse dunking tank had a clown perched on the bench with a microphone head set so he could bark at the crowd in hopes of getting them to spend money. However this clown was no hometown carnival heckler—he was just plain nasty. I mean really nasty. He was calling people names, swearing, making fun of people's mothers. Nasty, nasty, shit. But funny—think Andrew Dice Clay in a clown suit.

So here we come walking by Mr. Funny Pants, and he starts busting my balls about my long hair. Big deal. Everyone had long hair back then so it didn't really resonate. Then he says this one line and everything went sideways. He called my buddy Mike "Mr. Biker 90210." There was a collective gasp from the crowd and Mike stopped dead in his tracks. Well, that's the worst thing he could have done because it just egged on the clown into his whole routine.

Mike is no rube by any stretch of the imagination. He's a biker, father, and a successful businessman. One thing that Mr. Funny Pants didn't know about Mike was that he can throw a fastball right down the middle. Having no choice but to retaliate, Mike stepped up to the guy in charge of selling balls, three for a dollar, and threw a $20 bill down, which got him 60 balls.

The rest of us immediately got what he was going to do, so Ronnie, Darryl, and I also threw down $20. That was 240 balls to throw between four guys. Of course, the guys selling the balls threw in some extra balls. We all picked up the balls and like a rapid machine gun we let them fly, literally three and four at a time nonstop.

Instantly, one hit the target and the clown went in the water. But that didn't slow him down. He hopped right back up on his perch. As soon as he was in position, BANG, we hit the target again and he plunged back into the water. It was becoming quite a spectacle, a huge crowd started to gather, and we were not letting up. Hit, dunk, hit, dunk, hit, dunk, over and over. The clown was in and out of the water a

TIP:

Pay attention to the appearance of the cop–it could let you know just how much trouble you are in for. If he starts admiring your bike, you can relax a bit, but if you can see the reflection of your bike in his spit-polished boot, make sure you call him "Sir." If he's wearing a cowboy hat, especially when it is not an official part of his uniform, call your lawyer.

dozen times within minutes. However, this bastard still found the breath to call Mike "Mr. Biker 90210," rag on my long hair, and tell the other guys they threw like girls. It was amazing. We were dunking this guy every few seconds after he got back into position and he was still full of himself.

Enough clowning around

Now the crowd was really getting into it, and they started to cheer and yell. The clown started getting more and more obscene, and suddenly we were down to our last few balls. Mr. Funny Pants realized he had survived the barrage of balls and massive dunking, and he was still full of piss and vinegar. That's when we broke out the $100s. We came up with $300 and bought every single ball the booth had. We wanted 1,000 throws.

> **"That's when we broke out the $100s. We came up with $300 and bought every single ball the booth had. We wanted 1,000 throws."**

Mr. Funny Pants was going to shut the fuck up one way or another. However, we were getting tired. So Ronnie decided to invite every person standing around us to grab a ball and join in. That's when the shit really came unglued. There must have been 20 or 30 people humming balls at the targets and hitting one after the other.

Mr. Funny Pants was swallowing water by the gallons, and every so often when he could haul himself back up on the bench someone would hit the target and, splash, he was right back in the water. This went on for a good 20 minutes. The guy manning the booth was laughing his ass off and just feeding us extra balls as fast as he could. Pretty soon, the evil clown couldn't speak, couldn't catch his breath, and was almost drowning. So, of course, we started ragging on him; it was the best role reversal ever.

Finally, Mr. Funny Pants crawled/swam over to the side and climbed out the back of the tank. Game over. I swear, for the next year or two when he saw us coming he went on his break. Today, there's no longer a dunk tank at the Iron Horse and I would like to think that our little "drown the clown" episode had something to do with it.

Regardless, the moral of the story is simple: Clowns don't belong at bike rallies in the first place.

Just getting warmed up.

BIKEOLOGY:
The Perfect Day at Daytona Bike Week

- ☠ Wake up at 9 a.m., make coffee.

- ☠ Send the newest guy in the group to get bacon and egg sandwiches for everyone.

- ☠ Eat, drink coffee, and smoke a cigarette.

- ☠ Jump on your bike.

- ☠ Ride the Loop. The Loop is approximately 22 miles and it takes the rider through incredible tree-covered forests and along beautiful waterways. It begins at the Granada Bridge on John Anderson Drive in Ormond Beach, and then through a series of winding roads and turns taking you back where you started, hence the name the Loop. It's a must when riding in Daytona; however, do it early in the day so you can see everything.

Darryl and Ronnie getting ready for the perfect day.

- ☠ Head back and stop at Bruce Rossmeyer's Daytona Harley-Davidson across the street from the "Battle Grounds." Rossmeyer's Daytona Harley-Davidson is the largest Harley dealership in the world. The building itself is 109,000 square feet. The property has numerous vendors, bars, hotels, and concert stages. Pretty much something for everyone.

- ☠ Ride down the road to the Iron Horse Saloon.

- ☠ Ride over to Main Street. Hang out there. Any place is cool.

☠ Stop at the Ocean Deck off A1A for the crab legs (the Alaskan Trawler, as it's called on the menu).

☠ Go back to the house. Chill, shower, and drink, drink, drink.

☠ Call a cab and take it over to the Pink Pony or Lollipops.

☠ Drink, smoke, and watch strippers.

☠ Call a cab and head back over to Main Street.

☠ Drink.

☠ Call a cab and go home.

☠ Drink, bullshit, and tell stupid stories.

☠ Pass out around four or five, or watch the sunrise on the beach.

☠ Wake up the next morning and repeat the above, changing the riding destination and the bars.

☠ You could literally do this day all week and not get bored.

Sturgis Bike Week
Date: Second week in August
Location: Sturgis, South Dakota

Ahh! Sturgis Bike Week. This is, by far, my favorite rally and the best part of the country to ride in. Daytona is a great party, but Sturgis is the place for riding! The first year I went to Sturgis was 1996. By then I had figured out the house thing and how to ship my bike. I was more prepared for how to get there. But what I wasn't prepared for was the pure beauty of the landscape. I've started this chapter several times, but each time I would get so overwhelmed with all of the things I have to say about Sturgis that I found myself frustrated at a lack of proper words to describe it. So I decided to take a deep breath and start at the beginning.

My First Sturgis Trip

The first time I came to Stugis, I walked out into the airport parking lot and was immediately overwhelmed by the bright blue clear sky. It was stunning, and I'm not the kind of guy to say that very much, you know what I mean? The next thing that hit me was the smell of the air. The only way to describe it is clean. The other guys must have noticed the same thing because no one said a word. We just hopped into a shuttle van and headed over to an old airplane hanger where our trusty bike hauler Randy had our bikes polished up and ready to go.

We jumped on our bikes and hit the road. I have never felt freer on a bike than at that very moment. There's no helmet law in Sturgis, so none of us wore one. The perfect temperature combined with the clean-smelling air and blue sky and the vast wide-open space was purely spiritual. The ride from the airport to the town of Sturgis was only 30 or 40 miles, but it already ranked up

"The ride from the airport to the town of Sturgis was only 30 or 40 miles, but it already ranked up there with one of the best rides of my life."

there with one of the best rides of my life. Little did I know that the absolute best rides of my life were going to happen in the upcoming week.

Pulling into town

Nearing the exit for Sturgis, I remember smelling smoke from the surrounding campgrounds and seeing the traffic slow down to a complete stop as hundreds of bikers lined up and waited to exit. The best word I can use to describe the whole scene is "pure."

"My first piece of advice is to get a rally map and take the rides and routes that are clearly marked and suggested."

When I finally got off the exit and entered town, I realized that it was nothing more than a very small unassuming place in the middle of pretty much nowhere. The five of us pulled into the dirt parking lot of the real estate office, picked up the keys for the rental house, and snaked through some residential neighborhoods until we finally found it. It was perfect. It had a great view, was a mile from Main Street, and had a big garage. Honestly, I can't remember much more about that first day, but what I did know was that Sturgis, South Dakota, spoke to me. It was everything I had ever imagined about being part of the American motorcycle culture, and I had only been there for about two hours.

As in Daytona, much of what I'm about to tell you about happened over a 10-year span. However, before I get into the antics and craziness, I have to talk a little about riding. For the first few years, I remember not caring about where I was going to ride. At the beginning of the day, one of the guys would just pick a direction and we'd head out that way. The reason we did this was because when you look at the landscape of Sturgis you can see for miles. There are roads that literally cut across wide stretches of farmland, with huge bales of hay and old barns dotting the topography. So you can't head in a bad direction.

However, many of these secondary roads, although beautiful from a distance, end or turn to gravel. So my first piece of advice is to get a rally map and take the rides and routes that are clearly marked and suggested. These routes are all spectacular, and you won't get caught unexpectedly slipping around on gravel, getting hit in the face by rocks thrown off the guy's rear tire in front of you, or chipping your paint for miles.

Another advantage of having a map (and you can get maps anywhere in town for free) is that it highlights all of the national monuments. I think I heard once that there are more national parks and monuments in this part of the country than anywhere else. If that's not true, it sure feels like it is.

Some Places I Recommend Around Sturgis

Darryl, Ronnie, and me in front of Mount Rushmore.

www.nps.gov/moru

We found a friend while riding through Custer State Park. He moved toward Mark as he took this photo, and man, I have never seen a dude kick-start a Harley so fast.

www.sdgfp.info/parks/regions/custer/index.htm

Entering Devils Tower.

www.nps.goc/deto

The Badlands.

www.nps.gov/badl/

Me, Mark, and Mike
in front of Crazy Horse
just as the project was started.

www.crazyhorse.com

It's a beautiful view as the sun sets but don't forget to bring a set of clear lenses and a jacket.

I have been to Sturgis nine times so far and I promise you cannot see everything in just one visit. You might be able to ride through all of these places if you push it, but you really need to stop, relax, spend some time, and take it all in. I swear you can feel the spirits of the indigenous Indian tribes, pioneers, cowboys, and all that poetic shit you've learned about in high school. It's mystical. OK, I think I have made my point without sounding too much like Hemingway. So, go to Sturgis as many times as you can and ride around that part of the country as much as you can. It's that simple.

My Favorite Place

If you take only one ride in Sturgis, make it the Badlands. The Badlands are what I can only describe as prehistoric. I believe it covers more than 400,000 square acres. You first spot the Badlands when you are about 30 miles away and, honestly, you're not quite sure what the big deal is. It looks like a typical Midwest landscape with a bunch of bluffs and plateaus sticking up out of the ground. But as you get closer, you realize that it's a land that time forgot. As you enter the park you are greeted by sweeping curved roads, and around every turn is a new and spectacular sight.

The first time the boys and I rode through the Badlands, we must have stopped no less than 15 times. My speed-freak friends would turn into stunt men, literally. They would climb out onto small ridges that were only a few feet wide with several-hundred-foot drops. If you slipped off one of these peaks you weren't going home, ever. At each step my speed-junkie friends, now turned adrenaline junkies, kept handing me the

Mark, Darryl, and Ronnie—they might look like they are good friends but they're really hanging on to each other for dear life!

Darryl paid me to use this photo.

"If you slipped off one of these peaks, you weren't going home, ever."

That's a long fall.

camera and running out as far as they could on the narrowest peaks they could find. Yes, I took most of these photos from a safe distance. That's why I'm not in any.

It is as crazy as it looks. I do not recommend you try this . . . even though the photos are awesome.

We must have fucked around for hours that first year because as we exited the park it was getting dark. Normally this isn't a big deal, but like the lesson of the gravel roads, I was about to learn another little fact about riding in South Dakota. During the day temperatures often start out in the 80s or 90s, and then literally as soon as the sun goes down over the horizon, it plummets into the 50s or even 40s. So here we were, all amped up from seeing the most incredible state park in the world, it's getting dark, and we are more than 100 miles from town. No one has clear glasses or jackets and suddenly it's 45 degrees. Add the wind chill and the sunburn because we were much too cool to wear sunscreen (I do now), and you go from pure riding bliss to pure riding hell.

I took off my sunglasses because there were no streetlights and my eyes just started pouring tears. All of us were freezing. At some point, we pulled over and smoked a cigarette thinking that would help us get warm, and that's when we devised a plan.

A simple (stupid) plan

The plan was simple, but not very smart. We would get behind an 18-wheeler to block the wind and cold. It sounded pretty good at the time. We all pulled back on the road and took off trying to find an 18-wheeler to draft.

"Add the wind chill and the sunburn because we were much too cool to wear sunscreen (I do now), and you go from pure riding bliss to pure riding hell."

The other thing we didn't realize was that the speed limit in South Dakota is 75 miles per hour, so the truck had to be doing about 80 to 90 miles per hour. See what I'm getting at? We had to match the speed of the 18-wheeler at 80 miles per hour and then stay with it. So there we are, five guys hauling ass, doing between 85 and 90 miles per hour.

BIKEOLOGY:
Drafting

When you get behind or right on the side of another moving vehicle and use it to block the wind.

TIPS:
What to Do (and Not Do) in the Badlands

- ☠ Definitely ride through the Badlands, no matter what.

- ☠ Do not climb out on the narrow plateaus.

- ☠ Bring clear glasses, a jacket, chaps, a sweater, etc., even if you don't think it will be dark by the time you leave.

- ☠ Do not, under any circumstances, use an 18-wheeler to shield you from the cold.

- ☠ We were freezing.

- ☠ We couldn't see.

- ☠ We had no helmets.

- ☠ We were within a foot or two of a 10-ton 18-wheeler trying to stay warm.

The most obvious problem was that if the trucker hit his brakes, SPLAT, it would be like five bugs hitting a windshield. Darryl was actually so close that he reached out and put his hand on the trailer as he rode. I was pretty happy that no one fell to their death in the Badlands, but even more thankful when all of us made it home alive. I did end up with pneumonia that year and missed a week of work. I'm sure it was from that ride.

Racing the sun

I remember one time when we were caught leaving the Badlands with the sun going down. We raced the sun as it set, knowing that it would get cold fast. I, of course, could not keep up with the rest of the pack even though I had my speedometer buried at around 120 miles per hour. Ronnie and Darryl blew me away and made the 100-mile ride in less than 60 minutes. The sun was dipping below the horizon as we pulled into the driveway at the house.

In and Out

There are a few ways to ride to the Badlands. One year we managed to go in the back way. How, I have no idea. But as we approached, we passed through a little town called Interior. Now when I say little, I mean little. The whole place consisted of a few trailers on an Indian reservation. As we entered the town, we saw a little shack on the side of the road with big sign that said "BAR," but that's not where we pulled over. We pulled over on the left side of the road into a dirt parking lot with an even smaller adobe shack. Why, I have no idea.

This place was just plain strange. Inside we saw a big American Indian behind the bar, obviously the owner. I noticed that the whole place was powered off a single orange extension cord that ran from the adjacent trailer park about 100 yards away. The beverages of choice consisted of a few cases of beer crammed into a cooler on the side of the bar. Creepy but cool, in a Quentin Tarantino—movie kind of way.

Yes, Mark, this is all there is.

Of course, we decided to hang out for a while. As it turned out, the guy who was running the place was also living there and using the pool table as a bed. I couldn't make this shit up. So me and my buddies and the giant Indian dude, who looked straight out of *One Flew Over the Cuckoo's Nest*, sat around shooting the shit. Then, just when I thought I had it all figured out, a guy and his wife who were about 80 years old cruised in driving a Packard that was also about 80 years old.

So now there are eight people hanging out: Five bikers, a huge Indian, and two very senior citizens. Welcome to Bike Week. It was 100 degrees. There was no fan or air-conditioning, but there were lots of flies. We enjoyed that experience so much it naturally became a regular stop for us every year and the setting for these next three misadventures.

Hairspray

The bar across from the bar in Interior became a regular stop for the guys and me when we went to Sturgis. One year, as we pulled into the dirt-patch parking lot, I noticed a person standing in the doorway kind of hanging out. As I approached the entrance, this

"I noticed that the whole place was powered off a single orange extension cord that ran from the adjacent trailer park about 100 yards away."

person became clearer to me, but I still wasn't sure if it was a he or a she—as it turned out it was a little of both. I consider myself an open-minded guy. Who am I to judge? But this person was really off.

"As I approached the entrance, this person became clearer to me, but I still wasn't sure if it was a he or a she—as it turned out it was a little of both."

When our group got within 20 feet of the doorway, this cat, who was actually a man but obviously wanted to be a woman, came prancing over to us saying, "You boys want to buy me a drinkie?" That about freaked us all out pretty good. After we stopped laughing, we told our new pal to chill out and he/she went about picking up cigarette butts off the ground and smoking whatever was left of them.

I found out from the bartender that his/her name was Ralph and he was harmless. Ralph stood about 5 feet 10 inches tall and maybe weighed 100 pounds. He had on some kind of tube top, short daisy duke cutoffs, and ratty old sneakers. His legs were covered with hundreds of mosquito bites; his hair was jet black and looked like a bad Halloween wig that stuck up in a million spots.

Eventually Ralph took off, but about 10 minutes later he was back and this time he had a brown paper bag and can of hairspray with him. Now, I know a little about getting high. And throughout my life I've tried a little of this and sometimes a lot of that. But this was my first real exposure to huffing, or inhaling aerosol chemicals to get high. Needless to say, huffing is one of the cheapest and most disgusting ways to catch a buzz and it definitely causes permanent brain damage.

The old man's Packard. I think this was the only car ever at this bar.

Now we had crazy transvestite Ralphie, all dolled up, running around spraying his hair, spraying the hairspray into the paper bag, and then inhaling it. So this freak is as high as a kite asking us every five minutes if we can give him a cigarette and buy him a drink. At one point it just became pure comedy. The guy was pretty much completely lost in space.

Ronnie, who is the comedian of the group, thought it was time to have a little fun with Ralph. When Darryl went into the bathroom (and I use the word bathroom loosely), Ronnie gave Ralph a cigarette and told him that Darryl had been eyeing him up and down, but was too shy to tell him himself. He told Ralph that Darryl was hoping he would follow him into the bathroom. Ralph almost pissed himself he was so excited and, taking the bait, he wasted no time and ran into the bathroom.

"Now we had crazy transvestite Ralphie, all dolled up, running around spraying his hair, spraying the hairspray into the paper bag, and then inhaling it."

The rest of us sat and waited. It was dead silent for about two minutes and then we heard Darryl scream: "What the fuck are you doing . . . Hey . . . wo . . . get away from me." Darryl came running out of the bathroom holding up his pants, screaming. Ralph came out right behind him with a big grin, spraying his hair with his hairspray like a movie star getting ready for a big scene. The comic timing and the complete visual couldn't have been scripted better. Of course, Darryl cursed us out for a while, but after he calmed down, even he had to admit it was pretty funny.

I have been back to the bar across from the bar several times, but I have never seen Ralph again. I believe the legend of Ralph, the transvestite junkie who has a thing for bikers, is alive and well. So beware when you pull off the road in the remote little town of Interior and smell hairspray. Ralph might be right around the corner.

Meet the Flintstones

This story has to do with the 80-year-old guy, his wife, and their Packard. One year I thought it might be cool to take the old car for a ride, so I bought the guy a drink and asked him if I could take a spin. He knew me from the previous year and said sure. The car has a three on the column transmission, and the clutch was all messed up, but he gave me very specific and detailed instructions so I felt pretty comfortable. My plan was to take a quick spin around the reservation trailer park and come back. The car looked so cool I had to take it for a ride.

Bobby, one of the guys, said he'd come along, so we both hopped in. I started the car. No problem. Put it in first gear. No problem. Pulled out onto the dirt road. No problem. Shifted it into second gear. No problem. Hit the brakes to slow down. Big problem!

I was doing about 20 miles per hour down this dirt road, picking up speed, and right in front of me coming up fast was the jail. I knew it was a jail, not because it

"I had no brakes, and if there was any oncoming traffic, we were dead."

was a 10 by 10 adobe shack with one window that had three bars over it, but because the word "jail" was crudely hand-painted on it. Seriously, it looked like a jail from a Yosemite Sam cartoon. The last thing we wanted to do was blast through the wall in this old Packard, so I cut the wheel hard left. There was no power steering, so I mean *hard* left. Both Bobby and I screamed like little girls and missed the jail. However, we were heading out to the main road again and I was freaking the fuck out. I had no brakes, and if there was any oncoming traffic, we were dead. I closed my eyes and turned the wheel hard left again, avoiding the main highway.

Suddenly I realized that we had made a complete circle and we were heading back to the bar again. I still couldn't stop, get the car to downshift, or even stall the engine. There was just too much momentum—the entire trip was all downhill. We were out of control.

Pretty much in a panic now, I opened the door and stuck my leg out thinking I could actually stop the car a' la Fred Flintstone. Bobby must have thought it was a good idea because he did it too. I really wanted to jump out, but I couldn't bear

The old man and Bobby, still friends.

fucking up the only car the old-timer ever owned. The dust was flying! Bobby and I were hanging out each side of the car carving our heels deeper and deeper into the earth.

"He just smiled and said, 'Oh hell, I forgot. I drove about 70 miles to town the other day and got so used to it I plumb forgot.'"

After about 100 yards of these shenanigans I actually felt the car start to slow, and we were just about back to where we started, right in front of the bar. As luck would have it, we rolled down into an indent in the gravel parking lot and then up the other side. By then the car had lost its momentum and just rocked back and forth to a complete stop.

Bobby and I looked at each other in amazement, got out of the Packard and walked over to the old man. I was pissed and said, "I'm glad you told me about every fuckin' feature on the car and how to drive it, but why didn't you tell me there were no brakes?"

He just smiled and said, "Oh hell, I forgot. I drove about 70 miles to town the other day and got so used to it I plumb forgot."

I immediately got over being pissed and said, "My friend, there is a lot of shit you could have forgotten to tell me about the car, but forgetting to tell me that there weren't any brakes is a major fucking thing to forget." And that was that. We had a few more beers and took off into the Badlands. I saw the old guy and his car once more after that, but I think both he and his Packard are driving down that great big highway in the sky by now.

Bike in a bar

Albert was one of the guys who rode from Jersey to Sturgis. This was his first year at Sturgis and I was pretty excited to take him to the bar across from the bar. Once we arrived, the scene was pretty much the same except for a new owner, a few more chairs and tables, and two other bikers in the bar: a guy and his girlfriend. I guess word of mouth really spread on this hot spot.

We all got to talking and laughing, and the new owner got into the mix. After about an hour of BSing, someone brought up the subject of doing burnouts. Wanting to show off, I got into the gravel parking lot, fired up my scooter, and ripped out a burnout, which was pretty stupid because my back tire just dug into the ground and shot rocks everywhere. Of course, everyone else got in on the action and pretty soon dirt and gravel were flying everywhere.

However, no one could really get tires to smoke. So the bar owner told us we could pull our bikes into the bar and do burnouts inside. Understand that fitting a bike inside this bar would be a feat to defy physics. Realizing this, Ronnie and I put our back tires on the concrete sidewalk in front and lit 'em up. Smoke filled the bar. Everyone started yelling (all eight of us).

The owner was totally getting into it, so he told us that he really wanted someone to pull inside the bar and do a burnout on the carpet. The guy who was with his girlfriend said he could do it, and this bastard got his bike through the front door and past a pole in the middle of the bar, clearing it by inches. He turned his bike around in grand fashion and lit up the back, leaving a huge black spot in the middle of the carpet.

This was when Ronnie started egging Albert on.

Al positioned his bike at the right angle to get through the door, let out the clutch, and blasted in the bar. But just as we thought he would make it, the handlebars clip the support pole and down he went. Going down wasn't that big a deal, but because the bar was so small and the angles were so sharp, Albert became physically wedged between the pole and the bar. At first it seemed funny, but that changed when we realized that his throttle was stuck wide open.

So now "funny" became "dangerous" and none of us could figure out how to get the bike off Albert without getting chewed up in the back wheel. I kept yelling "Hit the kill

Not so impressive.

He made it look easy.

switch." Finally he did. It still took us 10 minutes to pry him out. While we were helping Al, I promised not to take any pictures—but I never said I wouldn't have a picture drawn of it.

Five Lights Are Better than One

Mark was the only guy in our group who rode an old Shovelhead. Now, I have nothing against Shovelheads except that they are not as reliable as the newer Evo models. If you own a Shovelhead you need to be a good mechanic.

"The five of us stood around while Mark insisted he could fix the problem in minutes. Of course, that took an hour."

Me coming through one of the caves carved through the mountain at the top of Needles.

Nothing personal against Mark, but every time we all take a trip together shit goes flying off his bike or we're stopping every 20 miles to fix it. Mark continually breaks one of the so-called rules I went over earlier: Don't rebuild your bike or do any major work right before you go to a major rally without putting on a few hundred test miles.

One day, while riding around Sturgis, the inevitable happened. A bolt flew off here, a nut there, etc. Pretty much shit flew off the bike everywhere, but nothing seemed to stop the bike from running, so we kept on going.

Later that evening we found ourselves in Rapid City, which is about 40 miles out from Sturgis. It was about 8 p.m. and all we wanted to do was head back to town and party, so we hopped on the highway and hit it. About a minute into the ride I noticed that Mark was pulling over, so of course the rest of us pulled over to see what the problem was. It turned out that the miscellaneous nuts and bolts that had been flying off Mark's bike earlier were mostly his electrical system—that meant he had no lights. The five of us stood around while Mark insisted he could fix the problem in minutes. Of course, that took an hour.

Finally, we all had enough and told Mark that he should just jump on the back of one of our bikes and we would come back and get his bike later with a trailer. Mark wasn't going for it. In warp speed he bolted everything back on the bike. Lo and behold, it fired up. Everything but the headlight worked, but that was still a big issue. There was no way we were waiting for him to check all of the wiring, so we came up with a plan. We would surround him and create a circle so he could use our headlights to see where he was going. This didn't sound like it would work to me, but I went with it (it was safer than drafting an 18-wheeler to stay warm).

We got into position and took off, all of us in one lane, two guys in front, one on each side of him, and one guy in back. Unbelievably, the damn plan worked out. We rode all the way back to Sturgis without incident. So, from this unexpected improvised plan, I can tell you that if you're with a few guys and someone loses a headlight, this works.

Mark's Revenge

So now that I've busted Mark's balls about all of the shit falling off his Shovelhead and how unreliable older bikes are, I think it's only fair to tell this story. Needles Highway is one of the most scenic and beautiful rides you can take. Most of the road winding up the mountain is a single lane with sharp switchbacks and crazy, steep, sloping twisties, and a lot of natural tunnels carved out of the natural rock formations. It's spectacular. It's definitely for the experienced rider though because you'll constantly be clutching and braking.

As we started our ascent, I saw Ronnie glide over to the side. He had blown his clutch. To be exact, he broke his clutch rod. That's the rod that goes in and out, engaging and releasing the clutch as you pull the clutch lever. Therefore he couldn't use the clutch to shift into gear. Needles is pretty far from Sturgis and we really wanted to do the ride. Mark is a very experienced rider. He offered to power shift Ronnie's bike for the rest of the ride.

Power shifting

Power shifting is definitely not something I recommend for the novice rider, especially on a road like Needles Highway. Ronnie and Mark switched bikes and off they went. Mark was doing a pretty good job and I thought for sure everything would be cool. We made it about a quarter of the way up and we were hitting some pretty tight switchbacks when suddenly I heard the bike rev and rev without moving.

Mark rolled over to the side of the road, which was extremely narrow, and the rest of us tucked in as close to the edge as we could. I went over to see what the problem was and by first glance everything seemed fine. That's when Ronnie walked over carrying his snapped belt drive. I have never actually seen a belt break.

BIKEOLOGY:
Power shifting

When you switch gears without using the clutch. The trick is to hear and feel the right rpms of the motor so when you shift the bike into gear it goes in smoothly.

TIP:

Always carry the number of a service center or roadside assistance service with you. There are companies at rallies that offer this service; just look around and you'll find one. Also, if you have AAA, check and see if you have motorcycle coverage.

This is what we looked like on the way up.

Above: Ronnie making the best of things, posing with the broken belt.

Right: Hope this doesn't happen in front of you when you are trying to coast to the bottom.

What I concluded was that because the bike had to be power shifted, extra tension was being put on the belt and eventually it snapped. When your belt drive snaps, that's it. You're dead in the water. I do believe that they make a quick repair kit for such a circumstance now, but they didn't back then.

The only solution: Turn around and go downhill. Remember, he had no clutch, so he had to put the bike in neutral and coast down the 10 miles we just rode up. That might not seem hard, but it is and here's why: You have to brake properly, especially through the flat parts and inclines or you'll lose momentum and come to a complete stop. There are hairpin turns, so your natural instinct is to slow way down and then simply accelerate out. You can't do that when you're coasting.

Because Ronnie had some years under his belt, he made it all the way down to the bottom and right into the visitors' center parking lot without a hitch. Once there, we called a towing service to come out and pick up the bike. Yes, we actually had a number for a towing service on us.

If we had not had that phone number, we would have had to ride all the way back to town, find a tow truck, and waste an entire day. Within two hours a guy showed up with a flatbed, loaded the bike, and said he would bring it to the local Harley dealer to get the belt and clutch fixed. Amazing. Ronnie was so happy with the way things turned out, he wanted to stay with us and ride, so Mark offered to let Ronnie ride on the back for the rest of the day.

Ronnie jumped on and we continued through Needles Highway and Custer State Park. At some point Ronnie turned around on the seat, rested against the backrest, and started taking pictures facing backwards. All in all, it worked out pretty damn good. We all had a great ride, and Ronnie's bike was fixed by the next morning.

Toothless

One year on the plane ride out to Sturgis, I met a few guys and started bullshitting and drinking with them. Of course the conversation revolved around how we expected the upcoming week to include much riding and partying. One of the guys reached in his pocket and pulled out a handful of pills. Jokingly, he said he had something for every occasion: Valium, Xanex, Percocet, etc. I laughed it off and after we got off the plane that was the last I saw of them . . . or so I thought.

This was the way down.

Taken off the back of Mark's bike.

After one full day of riding we were back at the house bullshitting . . . nothing out of the ordinary. Suddenly Mark sneezed, grabbed his mouth, sat up, and walked out of the room. Two minutes later when he came back we noticed he was missing a tooth, and not any tooth, one of his front teeth. He sneezed so hard he actually blew his cap right off.

Of course, we were a bit fucked up, and the sight of our buddy sitting there with no front tooth trying to talk was hysterical. He sounded like Cindy Brady from *The Brady Bunch* episode when she lost her tooth and spoke with a lisp. Then Ronnie, ever the comedian, got up, went into the kitchen, and came back holding his mouth and faked a sneeze blowing five sugar cubes out of his mouth across the room.

OK, so maybe you had to be there. But my point is we had several good hours of harassing toothless Mark. The next day when we went riding, he was not a happy camper. He looked like a hillbilly and was the brunt of every toothless joke we could make.

As he rode, the wind rushed directly onto the exposed nerve, causing extreme pain. Unable to enjoy himself, he decided to find a local dentist. Remarkably he did. Within a few hours he was as good as new. I honestly thought that because we were in Sturgis

"Suddenly Mark sneezed, grabbed his mouth, sat up, and walked out of the room. Two minutes later when he came back we noticed he was missing a tooth, and not any tooth, one of his front teeth. He sneezed so hard he actually blew his cap right off."

during Bike Week he was doomed and would end up looking like someone shoved a Chiclet into his mouth, but the dentist he found in the Yellow Pages did a great job.

At the end of the trip when we got on the plane to head home, I ran into the same guys I flew in with—the ones with the bag of pills. I had to tell them the tooth story. What I heard next trumped Mark's incident five times over.

Painkillers and alcohol

It seems my Pillbilly friend met a girl one night. The young lady invited him to her house just outside of town for a little nightcap. He said sure and hopped on his bike to follow. Of course, he was loaded on a combination of painkillers and alcohol. As he followed this chick through the backroads to her house the road turned into gravel. (I told you, that happens with a lot of roads in Sturgis, so beware.) He lost control of his bike and the next thing he knew he was in a ditch about 15 feet down on the side of the road.

Mark just trying to fit in.

He told me that when he hit the ground he smacked his mouth, but because he was so high, he didn't feel anything. I guess a few of his friends were behind him and they pulled him and his bike out of the ditch. After shaking off the fall he noticed that something in his mouth felt funny, and when he examined it further he found that he had knocked out five of his teeth!

> "He lost control of his bike and the next thing he knew he was in a ditch about 15 feet down on the side of the road."

But I was looking right at him and he seemed fine. I thought he was full of shit. Well, it seemed that he also found a dentist in the Yellow Pages who was willing and able to replace all of his missing teeth. They were a little whiter than his real teeth; other than that they looked perfect.

Then he triumphantly reached into his pocket, pulled out another bottle of painkillers, and said the rest of his week was great. He hooked up with the same chick the following night. Now that's tenacity. The bottom line: Beware of the backroads in Sturgis at night. They could turn into gravel in an instant.

Sturgis obviously has some really great dentists, who knew?

"The bottom line: Beware of the backroads in Sturgis at night. They could turn into gravel in an instant."

Arlen in Spearfish

When you take a bike trip like Sturgis, chances are you're going to see a bike builder or two that you really admire and respect, or a bike that just blows you away. In 1996, while I was in Sturgis, I decided to take a ride out to the town of Spearfish. Why? I don't know. But someone somewhere told me that it was a neat place. The only thing I thought was neat was the name, and then I saw the sign entering the town: literally, a giant fish with a spear through it, blood and all.

Anyway, I went with the guys to Spearfish and quickly realized the only thing to see was the salmon and trout farm. Why the fuck was I taking a tour of a fish farm during Bike Week? I mean, really, this was like the last thing I wanted to do.

"Why the f&#k was I taking a tour of a fish farm during Bike Week?"

Can you tell I wasn't really that thrilled about fish?

After about half an hour of looking at fish I had had enough, and so did everyone else. Time to hit the road. As we gathered our shit together and smoked a quick cigarette, I saw a truck pull into the cul-de-sac where we were parked. I couldn't see what was written on the side of the truck, only that a few guys were opening the back door and putting down a ramp. Because it was Bike Week, this is a pretty common sight. So I went about my business packing my saddle bags getting ready to leave when Ronnie turned to me as said "Hey, man. I think that's Arlen Ness!"

SmoothNess

I turned and saw a guy with a shock of white hair throwing a leg over a bike, then I saw he was riding *SmoothNess* in the bare metal finish before it was painted green. It was awesome. I could not believe I was in some cul-de-sac at a fish farm seeing Arlen Ness test ride one of the most influential and radical custom bikes ever built. I just stood there bewildered and watched him go up and down the street. Then his crew loaded the bike back into the truck and left.

"This proved to me that no matter where you go when you're in Sturgis, you never know who or what you might see."

Arlen Ness on *SmoothNess* before it was painted green.

This proved to me that no matter where you go when you're in Sturgis, you never know who or what you might see. Seeing *SmoothNess* when it was first built and seeing it being ridden by the guy who created it is definitely something I'll never forget. However, I have never been back to the fish farm.

Judge Judy

On one spectacular ride on my way to Wyoming to see Devils Tower, my pals and I passed through the town of Aladdin. Upon entering the town I noticed a sign that said "Population: 15." That's right, 15. So we had to pull over.

When you pull into Aladdin, you basically pull off the main road into a gas station/general store/town hall/bar/post office, all in one small building. I also noticed that there were at least 200 parked bikes and another 50 lined up at the gas pump.

"Upon entering the town I noticed a sign that said 'Population: 15.' That's right, 15. So we had to pull over."

Without any other choice, I went inside the gas station/general store/town hall/bar/post office and noticed a "For Sale" sign tacked up on a cork bulletin board. The town itself was being sold.

The sign read: "For Sale: Town of Aladdin, 17 acres including all buildings and gas station. $1.4 million."

I thought it was a novel idea but didn't take it seriously. Years later, right after I became the producer of *American Thunder*, I told my crew that I wanted to head out to Devils Tower and film it. Darryl (who has made every Daytona and Sturgis trip with me) reminded me that we were going to pass through Aladdin on our way and that we should stop just for the hell of it. When I pulled in, I saw that there were a few improvements and the place looked, I don't know, less broken down. I went inside and saw the same cork bulletin board and, sure as shit, I saw a new "For Sale" sign. The only thing different was that the price had gone up to $2 million.

"The sign read: 'For Sale: Town of Aladdin, 17 acres including all buildings and gas station. $1.4 million.'"

The town of Aladdin has the only gas pump for miles.

Good TV

This time I was curious to find out if this was for real and, if so, I had a few questions. I asked inside if anyone had more information about the town and, as luck would have it, I ran into one of the town's owners, Judy—an attractive, well-kept woman, maybe in her late 60s, who wore a pair of cowboy boots, Western-style shirt, and all topped off with a diamond-encrusted horseshoe necklace. She looked like someone who would own this town.

I asked Judy a few questions, and she was very cool. Actually, the story seemed like good TV so I decided to do a little segment for *American Thunder* about the town and how it thrived with all of us bikers stopping in during Bike Week. I interviewed Judy for about 20 minutes and learned she and her husband purchased the town 10 years prior. It covered 17 acres and there were a half dozen buildings included in the price. During Bike Week they made a bunch of money pumping gas because it was the only gas station between Sturgis and Devils Tower. In the winter they made a few bucks issuing hunting permits and setting up guided hunting tours. She wasn't only an owner of the town, but the mayor as well.

When I finished interviewing her, I asked her to give her best 10-second sales pitch, and she did. She was a very pleasant and good-natured woman. I liked her. Off camera I joked with her and said if I actually aired her little sales pitch, and someone bought the town because of it, I wanted a commission.

The crew wrapped and we rode out to Devils Tower. About two months later the Sturgis episode and the piece with Judy and Aladdin

"She looked like someone who would own this town."

made the show. It was a great segment. At the end of the segment, Judy did her sales pitch and that was that. Pretty good TV.

About a week later I received an e-mail from a fan asking me about contacting Judy so he could buy the town. A few weeks later I received another e-mail from the same guy thanking me and saying he had bought the town.

So, Judy, if you're reading this and holding my commission check, I'm pretty easy to find . . . just kidding. Most important, remember when you're heading out to Devils Tower, don't just fly by Aladdin. Stop by and gas up. You'll be glad you did. Who knows, maybe you'll be the next mayor—if the price is right, that is.

Ronnie, Darryl, and Me. I wonder if this tent counts as one of the buildings.

Bike? What Bike?

One night, our group hung out on Main Street until the last call. I believe we stayed in the same bar for something like 10 hours. These days, hanging out until last call in Sturgis during Bike Week is not a good idea. You will most likely have to pass through several drunk-driving checkpoints.

As the bars shut down, I separated from the group and headed out to where I thought my bike was parked. As I walked around the streets, I noticed a ton of cops checking me out, obviously observing if I was drunk and planning to get on my bike. This made me a little paranoid, so I straightened up and concentrated really hard on trying not to look like a drunken fool.

While I focused on acting sober, I lost track of where I was walking. I was so buzzed that I couldn't concentrate, maintain a sober facade, or find my bike. Ten minutes later I had no idea where I

"These days, hanging out until last call in Sturgis during Bike Week is not a good idea. You will most likely have to pass through several drunk-driving checkpoints."

was. I knew I was heading out of town and nowhere near my bike. I turned around and started walking in the opposite direction. It was hopeless. The cops were still hovering. I was up shit creek.

Another problem I had was that, up until about four or five years ago, cell phones didn't work for shit in Sturgis so I couldn't call anyone for help. At about 3 a.m., when I had given up all hope of finding my bike, I saw my friend Ray cruising by yelling, "Hey, Jay! Hey, Jay! Where are you going? Where have you been?"

BIKEOLOGY:
Riding bitch

Being the passanger on the back of a motorcycle, mostly reserved for women. Not exactly the manliest thing to do.

Riding bitch

Ray pulled over and I nonchalantly told him I had everything under control and that I was just heading over to my bike. Ray, who was sober, informed me that my bike was parked about a mile from where I was and I was heading in the wrong direction. So I, Mr. Tough Guy, said, "No problem, just tell me where to go and I'll walk there." Ray just laughed and told me to jump on the back of his bike and he would shuttle me. As drunk as I was, I still resisted riding bitch, but after a few minutes of standing on the sidewalk and feeling stupid, I said "Sure" and jumped on.

Ray's bike wasn't even a Harley. I think it was a Yamaha and basically the starter bike he had learned to ride before getting a Harley. Here we were, dressed in black leathers from head to toe because it was cold, Ray 6 feet 11 inches and weighing about 280 pounds and me 6 feet 2 inches weighing about 220 pounds, and we're both riding down Main Street on this little Yamaha. We looked like two guys from the Village People.

There were still a bunch of cops lingering, looking for guys just like Ray and me. As we putted by at about 5 miles per hour, I thought for sure we were going to get busted.

> "As drunk as I was, I still resisted riding bitch, but after a few minutes of standing on the sidewalk and feeling stupid, I said 'Sure' and jumped on."

But I was wrong. Instead of getting hauled off to jail, the cops just burst out laughing. Not really knowing what to do, I just waved back with one of those stupid parade style waves. That was all the cop could take because a few of them just about fell over laughing. Not cool.

Within a few minutes Ray had me at my bike and I rode home sobered by pure embarrassment.

Will the Real Kid Rock Please Stand Up?

This might be my favorite story, but there's a lot of setup, so bear with me. A few years ago when I went to Sturgis to film for *American Thunder*, I had a few of my friends join me there. Paul and Darryl had never met before, and the plan was for them to hook up in Wyoming at the airport, pick up their rented bikes from the Harley dealer in Casper, and ride out to meet me in Sturgis. I had warned Paul in advance that Darryl was a cop magnet and to be careful when riding with him.

About five o' clock that evening, they pulled into the hotel to meet me. (This was the first and only year I ever stayed in a hotel during Sturgis Bike Week.) When I went over to greet them, Paul just started laughing his ass off. Of course, Darryl got pulled over by the cops within the first 10 minutes they were on the road.

The three of us hung out for a while, had a beer, and then jumped on our bikes to head into town. Darryl and Paul were both riding Ultra Glides with full tour packs. I was riding a 9-foot-long chopper. We were no more than 200 yards out of the parking

"This cop must have been related to the guys who arrested Darryl in Holly Hill, Florida, several years ago, because he was wearing a huge cowboy hat, jeans, and carrying a bone-handled nickel-plated .357 Magnum."

lot when a cop hit his lights and pulled Darryl over for the second time in one day—something about rolling through a stop sign.

This cop must have been related to the guys who arrested Darryl in Holly Hill, Florida, several years ago, because he was wearing a huge cowboy hat, jeans, and carrying a bone-handled nickel-plated .357 Magnum. The cop asked Darryl to step off his bike and show him his driver's license. As Darryl went into his pocket and pulled out his wallet, two neatly folded $100 bills fell out onto the ground inches from the cop's polished cowboy boot. All of us looked down at the bills, then up at the cop. The silence was deafening.

Then Darryl looked right at the cop and said, "Hey, that's how we do it in Jersey." Just when I thought we were all going to jail, the cop just broke up laughing. Darryl calmly reached down and put the money back in his wallet. When the cop stopped laughing, he told us to hit the road. Strike two for D-man, but still no ticket.

TIP:

A water bottle is perfect for a little gas. You can buy a bottle of water, dump it out, then fill it with gas. Rinse it with gas first, or you'll get droplets of water in your tank. Not good. Or, if you have a water bottle, you can unhook your buddy's gas line from the petcock and get a little emergency reserve that way. Just remember what's in there when you suddenly get thirsty on the road.

Out of gas

That night we partied until about 2 a.m. and then headed back to our hotel in Whitewood. About a mile from the exit, I ran out of gas just as Paul and Darryl got off the exit. Fortunately my cell phone was working, so I waited a few minutes and called Paul, figuring he would be back at the hotel and notice I was missing. He picked up and I told him I was out of gas and needed him to get some gas to me.

I didn't expect his reply. Paul told me that a cop had Darryl pulled over at the top of the exit ramp and he was going to see what the problem was before coming to help me. I told him to just bring me the gas. It took Paul about 20 minutes to find me because the exits in Sturgis are sometimes 20 miles apart. He handed me the bottle of gas, and told me that he saw the cop handcuffing Darryl.

I dumped the gas into my bike, hopped back on, and the two of us headed to the scene where the cop had Darryl. By the time we got there, they were gone and a tow truck driver was getting ready to haul Darryl's bike away. We tried desperately to bribe

"Paul and I were exhausted and buzzed. The last thing we wanted to do was ride 40 miles to a police station, but we had to check on Darryl."

the guy to leave the bike, but he wasn't having any of it. He basically told us to fuck off and split before we got him into trouble. But he also said that if we wanted to find our friend, we should head over to the Deadwood jail. We could get the bike in the morning.

Paul and I were exhausted and buzzed. The last thing we wanted to do was ride 40 miles to a police station, but we had to check on Darryl. So I did the only thing I could. I went back to the hotel and woke up my cameraman. Yep, the cameraman who was shooting *American Thunder* for me. He was a trooper and agreed to help. So we all packed into the production van and headed over to the jail.

TIP:

It's always better to take a blood alcohol test rather than a breathalyzer test if you think you're borderline. The chances that the blood test will come back lower than a breathalyzer are good. You see, it takes about an hour after they arrest you to do the blood test, so you get more time to sober up.

Blood alcohol

When we pulled into the parking lot, the first thing I saw was a young woman in her pajamas wearing fuzzy bunny slippers walking into the jail. It was 4 a.m., so I just assumed that she was coming to bail a friend out. When I went inside, I found out she was the local nurse and she was there to test Darryl's blood alcohol level. You see, the overzealous cop who arrested him did so as Darryl was actually pulled over and at a complete stop on the side of the road with the motor turned off. Darryl knew he wasn't that buzzed so he declined the breathalyzer test and opted for a blood test.

It's always better to take a blood alcohol test rather than a breathalyzer test if you think you're borderline. The chances that the blood test will come back lower than a breathalyzer are good. You see, it takes about an hour after they arrest you to do the blood test, so you get more time to sober up.

While the nurse did the blood test, we all stood around trying to get Darryl released on a PTA. (PTA means "Promise To Appear" in court after you get arrested.) Even though most of the cops were laughing, and Darryl tried dropping a few hundred on the floor just as a gag, it was no luck and he was staying the night. All in all, the jail looked kind of quaint, like the one on *The Andy Griffith Show*. Darryl and I both thought that he would be sleeping in a comfortable cell and some little old lady, like Aunt Bea, would be bringing him breakfast in the morning. So Paul, my camera guy, and I left.

Full Throttle Saloon

This was Paul's first trip and first day in Sturgis, and so far he had three encounters with the law. I had a show to shoot in a few hours and I had to get some sleep, so I asked Paul to please go back to Deadwood in the morning to make sure Darryl got out of jail. A couple hours later I went to the Full Throttle Saloon to film a magenta, pink, and green chopper owned by a guy named Johnny Lange. The first thing everyone notices about Johnny is that he's the spitting image of Kid Rock. I worked with Kid once on a television show I used to produce and had seen him backstage at many other shows. When Johnny wears his cowboy hat and sunglasses, he's a dead ringer. I interviewed Johnny,

Me hard at work
interviewing Johnny.

Adam M. Umholtz

shot his bike, and found out that he was a very cool cat. After the interview we made plans to meet back at the Full Throttle and have a few drinks.

Also that day, while I was interviewing and filming Johnny, there were midget wresting matches going on. Yes, midget wrestling. It's the same as the WWE, but much smaller and, in my opinion, way more entertaining. Meanwhile, my poor friend Paul was stuck at the Deadwood courthouse waiting for Darryl to go in front of the judge so he could be released. At 6:30 that evening I finished shooting and drove back to the hotel. Paul and Darryl showed up 20 minutes later.

Darryl gets released

The night in jail didn't go exactly the way Darryl had hoped. After we left, the cops told Darryl to strip, gave him a jump suit, a rubber mat, and told him to sleep on the floor. When he woke up two hours later, he discovered he was in a cell filled with hardcore criminals. He told me that breakfast was very interesting and he was *encouraged* to share his grape jelly, which he did.

When his case came up in the courtroom, the D.A. looked at his file and told him that he should get a lawyer. His blood alcohol was only .001 over the legal limit. And because he was

"He told me that breakfast was very interesting and he was *encouraged* to share his grape jelly, which he did."

TIP:

Over the last few years both Sturgis and Daytona have really cracked down on driving while impaired during Bike Week in part becasue they make lots of money in fines.

stopped on the side of the road, there was a good chance that he could probably get out of a DUI. Darryl took the D.A.'s advice, got a lawyer, and sure enough, they let him off. Of course, he had to plea to a lesser charge, and when it was all said and done the state still got its $1,500, but Darryl didn't get a DUI. Over the last few years both Sturgis and Daytona have really cracked down on driving while impaired during Bike Week in part because they make lots of money in fines.

Darryl was pretty beat up from having only a few hours of sleep on a concrete floor, but he felt bad that Paul, a guy he hardly knew, wasted the entire day helping him get out of jail. Shit! Paul was only in town for a few days and one of them was already shot, so Darryl sucked it up and said he wanted to go out and party. Of course, Paul was psyched just to do something other than hang around jail. I told them that the plan was to meet up with Johnny and Patrick at the Full Throttle. What I didn't know was that the real Kid Rock was playing just up the road from the Full Throttle at the Buffalo Chip Campground. On the way there, we sat in traffic for hours. Things weren't off to a great start.

Local celebrity

A few minutes after we arrived, my friend Patrick showed up with a bunch of midget wrestlers. The bunch of us found a spot at the bar and ordered drinks. People definitely noticed us with the midgets, and many of them knew me from *American Thunder*.

Then my new friend Johnny called me from the front parking lot and asked if I could come out and walk him in. I said, "Sure, why not?" When I met him out front I noticed that he had the Kid Rock cowboy hat and sunglasses on, so we walked into the bar and that's when the fun started. The crowd around us parted and people started saying things like "Hey, there's Kid Rock." Then it dawned on me: The

Me and Patrick gearing up for the evening.

Adam M. Umholtz

"When I met him out front I noticed that he had the Kid Rock cowboy hat and sunglasses on, so we walked into the bar and that's when the fun started."

real Kid Rock had just finished playing up the road and most of the people from the concert were now filing in at the Full Throttle. The timing was unbelievable.

So here we are: Paul, Darryl, Patrick, and the midgets, hanging around a guy everyone thinks is Kid Rock. At that point, a guy we knew started taking pictures, moving around like he was some kind of professional photographer, and the flash was going off every two seconds. That really amped up the crowd. Within minutes there were no less than 50 drinks on the bar in front of us and a thousand or more people closing in to get a closer look. Because it was never Johnny's intention to pretend he was Kid Rock, all of us frantically started telling people that he wasn't Kid Rock, but the more we said he wasn't, the more people thought he was. People were actually saying with a wink, "Yeah right, I know you guys are just trying to play it down." I guess people believe what they want, no matter what.

The crowd gathers at the Full Throttle.

Adam M. Umholtz

Everyone thinks Johnny is Kid Rock no matter what we tell them.
Adam M. Umholtz

The front of the card.
Adam M. Umholtz

Finally, we all gave up and went with it. The midgets jumped up onto the bar and started dancing around, giving Jello shots to all the girls. There were people 50 deep standing on chairs taking pictures and posing with Johnny. It was surreal.

Then, out of the crowd, this 5-foot-nothing girl pushes her way over to Darryl. She tells him she was sorry that they had had to meet under unfortunate circumstances but she loves Kid Rock and could he please help her get a picture with him. Darryl, exhausted, drunk, and in the middle of a frenzy suddenly realizes that this girl is the D.A. from Deadwood who helped him get out of jail earlier that day. Not knowing what else to do he said "sure" and escorted her up to Johnny, who posed with her while flipping the bird.

The insanity went on for several more hours, and then finally Johnny snuck out just before the bar closed down. It was a pretty wild night, but not the end of the story. Four months later Darryl got a Christmas card in the mail. On the front was the picture of the D.A. with Johnny taken that night. Inside it reads:

Darryl,

I wanted to drop you a line and let you know that it was a pleasure meeting you. I'm just sorry it was under such unfortunate circumstances.

I don't make a habit of writing to "defendants" but wanted to let you know that working with you was very refreshing. I'm not usually greeted so pleasantly by individuals I've prosecuted, so it was nice to feel so welcomed when I saw you at the Full Throttle.

I also wanted to thank you for a great Rally memory and the opportunity to meet Kidd Rock! Meeting you both was truly the highlight of my very hectic week.

Take care and perhaps I'll end up running into you during the 2005 Rally, (hopefully not in Court!!!!).

If the D.A. from Deadwood is reading this, I'm sorry to kill your buzz. But this story was just too good not to tell.

Short Dawg, one of the midget wrestlers, administers a Jello Shot.
Adam M. Umholtz

CHAPTER SEVEN

ANY EXCUSE TO RIDE

As I said earlier, Laconia, Daytona, and Sturgis are the three major motorcycle rallies that happen annually. They are also the three that have been around the longest. It's a pretty good bet that they will be happening for many more years to come. However, if you can't make one of these rallies, there are a few others that are pretty good. My criteria for judging whether a rally is worth visiting is the following:

It must be established for more than 10 years. Start-up rallies are risky because they just don't get a good turnout. It takes years for word of mouth to spread and for rallies to become established. What makes bikers want to go to rallies are the stories they hear on the road and the chance to be around other bikers. You can walk up to almost anyone in the United States and ask him or her if they've heard of Sturgis Bike Week, and most will say yes. If you ask them what they know or have heard about it, they'll most likely say it's a wild place with thousands of bikers. The American motorcycle culture is built on storytelling and it doesn't matter whether it's done in the media, around a campfire, or the office water cooler. Bottom line: if you go to rallies that have been established for at least 10 years, there's a better chance of experiencing what the culture is all about.

Second, the attendance must be more than 25,000. The reason for this is simple: more people, more variety, and more bikes means more fun and more exposure to the culture.

Third, the rally must be held over a few days. There are no such things as one-day rallies. If it's one day, it's an event, cookout, pig roast, fundraiser, or party. A rally means multiple days, period.

Don't get me wrong, you should go to as many one-day local events as possible and check out all of the new events that you can. However, until you have been to Laconia, Daytona, or Sturgis, you have *not* had the rally experience.

A Few Rallies to Check Out

Laughlin River Run
Date: Last weekend in April
Location: Laughlin, Nevada

The Laughlin River Run is held every year in the tiny town of Laughlin, Nevada, about 60 miles south of Las Vegas right on the Arizona border. This is almost a major rally, but the attendance never gets to more than 100,000. Laughlin consists of a strip of casinos that run along the Colorado River. Sounds nice, but it's in the middle of nowhere and if you're going to be out in that part of the country you might as well go to Vegas.

> ". . . until you have been to **Laconia, Daytona, or Sturgis,** you have not had the rally experience."

Laughlin is a good run for bikers in the California, Las Vegas, and Arizona areas because you can ride there. Otherwise it's tough. You have to fly to Vegas, rent a bike, and then drive an hour. If you ride to Laughlin, you should start very early in the morning because the mid day temperatures can get well over the 100-degree mark.

There is one cool ride to take if you do go to Laughlin, and that's to the small mining town of Oatman, an old Western ghost town famous for the gold rush. But when the gold ran out, so did the people. Donkeys roam the streets freely and most of the original buildings are still there so it's pretty cool.

Overall, Laughlin is fun, cheap, and you can gamble all night on $100.

BIKEOLOGY:
Rally requirements

- ☠ Must be established for 10 years or more.

- ☠ The attendance must be more than 25,000.

- ☠ It has to last at least three days.

Las Vegas Bike Week
Date: Last weekend in September
Location: Las Vegas, Nevada

Obviously this event is in Las Vegas; however, it does not take place on the main strip. It is held downtown in the Fremont Street area. There is usually a pretty good bike show at this event and a lot of vendors. The only drawback is that it's more Vegas than bike rally. It's kind of hard to get the feel of the American motorcycle culture when you're surrounded by Sin City. Most of the participating bikers are from Las Vegas, California, and Arizona.

This is a good rally to do with your wife or girlfriend. You can get a room on the strip at one of the major luxury hotels and then buzz down to Fremont Street to party. This is the perfect trip to combine a vacation with a bike rally.

Biketoberfest
Date: Third weekend in October
Location: Daytona Beach, Florida

Biketoberfest is a spin-off rally from Daytona Bike Week in March. I have been to this rally a few times and it's always fun, probably because I'm so familiar with Daytona. There are two major differences between this rally and the one in March.

- ☠ Less people attend, so it's easier to get around.

- ☠ It's only three to four days, compared to the one in March, which is seven to 10 days.

- ☠ It's also more laid-back than the one in March.

I'm not sure why this rally ever got started. It has nothing to do with Halloween or a beerfest, and there is already a very successful and popular Bike Week there in March. But I like it and recommend it.

In the back are two of the hottest bartenders at the Full Throttle.
In front (left to right) are Me, Johnny, a guy who wanted his picture taken, Paul, and another random fella.

ROT Rally (The Republic of Texas)
Date: First weekend in June
Location: Austin, Texas

I discovered this rally a few years ago, which enforces another point about the American motorcycle culture—and that's discovery.

The reason I went to the ROT rally in 2006 was to film for *American Thunder* and I had no idea what to expect, except that it was established more than 10 years ago, lasts over three days, and there are well more than 25,000 bikers attending. Actually, over 100,000 bikers show up for this bash.

I arrived in Texas, climbed into my production car, and drove over to the rally to scout the site. That's when I got confused. Where were all of the bikes? There were no signs welcoming bikers. I started to think I had made a big mistake. After driving around Austin for an hour, I finally asked someone where the ROT rally was, and they gave me directions that led me about 20 minutes out of town. But after 10 minutes of driving, I still didn't see any bikes or signage. Fifteen more minutes into my journey, and still no bikes.

BIKEOLOGY:
Pig roast

A traditional biker party where a whole pig is roasted over an open pit for 10 to 12 hours and then eaten.

At other big rallies, there are signs for miles around stretched across streets, hanging on windows, on billboards, etc., that read "Welcome Bikers." There are also tons of people riding everywhere you look. So when I saw neither, I began to wonder what I was in for.

Then suddenly I saw three guys riding on Harleys. I followed them into what appeared to be the industrial business district of Austin. Then we made a few more turns and, bingo, I saw it: The ROT Rally. It was a mega fairground. There were several gated entrances spaced out over miles. Once I made it inside, I saw thousands of RVs and tents dotting the landscape spread out over hundreds of acres.

This rally is not about the vendors. It's about the freedom to be a biker.

The founders and promoters of the rally, Jerry Bragg and his wife, Colleen, told me that their philosophy is simple. They wanted to recreate the atmosphere of Sturgis the way it was 25 years ago. The cost to camp at this rally is almost nothing, which attracts a "live and let live" group. Bikers attend in million-dollar travel buses or just roll up on a bike with a sleeping bag.

Most of the fun comes from riding around the campgrounds, especially at night. There is a lot of nudity and many of the naked shouldn't be, know what I mean? People ride around in tricked-out golf carts, and the campfires burn brightly into the dawn hours.

There are several other rallies that meet my criteria, but as I said, a major part of this culture is about discovery. So guess what? You need to find out a lot of this stuff on your own. Ask other bikers, read biker magazines, or surf the Internet. The actual process of discovery will automatically make you more knowledgeable. And knowledge equals authenticity, the key ingredient to becoming part of the American motorcycle culture.

End of the Road

All and all, I wrote this book as a result of the recent insane growth of the American motorcycle culture. It's great that millions of people are getting into riding and hitting the highways, but it's not so great when they disrespect the authenticity of the culture. The old saying "keep it real" applies best to our community and in order to keep it real, you need to remember you can't buy your way in and you can't buy cool.

I sincerely hope you have enjoyed this book and that, at the end of the day, you will find yourself on a beautiful stretch of road with the wind in your face, the sun on your back, and everything about being part of the American motorcycle culture will suddenly become clear. That's the day you will realize that being a biker is never about the destination . . . it's only about the journey.

APPENDIX

Motorcycle Organizations, News, and Message Boards

Here are a few credible motorcycle organizations that you can join or just use as a resource. However, don't confuse being part of one of these groups and being in a motorcycle club…even if you can buy the giant three-piece back patch.

H.O.G (Harley Owners Group)

A great organization to join so you can learn about upcoming motorcycle events, local rides, etc. www.hog.com

ABATE (Depending on the state, the letters stand for "American Brotherhood Aimed Towards Education," or "American Brotherhood Against Totalitarian Enactments.")

Started in response to helmet laws, this organization will keep you updated on all current legislation and motorcycle laws. www.abate.org (This is the website for California, however almost every state has their own chapter.)

AMA (American Motorcyclist Association)

Their slogan is "Rights, Riding, Racing." If it has something to do with two wheels you'll find out about it here. www.amadirectlink.com

BADD (Bikers Against Drunk Driving)

Their name pretty much says it all. www.baddcentral.com

MSF (Motorcycle Safety Foundation)

You can find beginner and advanced riding classes in your area, get the latest news on legislation and laws in your state, safety tips, and a lot more. www.msf-usa.com

Ronnie Cramer's Motorcycle Web Index

This is a great central hub for all the major websites. You can find links to manufacturers, aftermarket companies, news, trading sites, riding tips, and a whole lot more. sepnet.com/cycle/

Bikernet.com

This site will pretty much tell you everything you need to know. It was started by Keith Ball, a biker who's been involved in the industry forever. www.bikernet.com.

Motorcycle Consumer News

Good industry news, road tests and product tests, and all-around good site to check regularly. www.mcnews.com/mcn/

American Rider

This is the online version of the magazine of the same name. Harley-specific articles, videos, news, and links to good apparel and parts companies. www.americanrider.com

Easyriders

This is the magazine's website and acts as a portal to many of the biker lifestyle magazines (including a number of tattoo mags). Checking a magazine's website is a good way to browse the content without getting kicked out of the store. www.easyriders.com

Hot Bike

Another Harley-centric magazine's website. You'll find a lot of news, photos, do-it-yourself projects, and links to good sources of info. www.hotbikeweb.com

Long Riders

This is a real grassroots biker magazine and website with lots of news about rallies, swap meets, clubs, bikes for sale, rides, and more. www.longridersmagazine.com

Motorcycle Daily

This is a general motorcycle industry news website. When a company releases a new product or a new bike, or there's a big race or event going on, you'll read about it here. www.motorcycledaily.com

Motorcycle USA

This news and info site has sections devoted to touring, customizing, and racing…all important areas of motorcycle news that any Harley owner will want to pay attention to. www.motorcycle-usa.com

Motorcycle.com

This is a good central nervous center for news and info. Sectioned by manufacturer, with info on gear, parts, insurance, financing, laws, and hot biker babes. Enjoy. www.motorcycle.com

Motorcyclist

The online version of the magazine. Road tests of bikes, parts, gear, apparel, etc. Plus all the industry news you'll need. A good source for any biker's needs. www.motorcyclistonline.com

Rider

Another online version of a magazine, this site has a great marketplace section for finding used bikes, reviews, parts, gear, etc. It also has a message board where you can communicate with fellow riders on a variety of subjects. www.ridermagazine.com.

Magazines

Some magazines are all about Harleys, choppers, and other customs. Some magazines cover the whole spectrum of motorcycling, from Harleys to Italian sportbikes. Some feature a lot of road tests and industry info, while others focus on hot pictures of custom builds and babes. The best advice I can give you is to spend some time at your local bike shop, bookstore, or library and browse some titles to see what fits your style. You can also check a magazine's website for a taste of what they offer and order a subscription.

Easyriders, www.easyriders.com/easyriders

American Iron, www.aimag.com

Cycle World, www.cycleworld.com

Rider, www.ridermagazine.com

Biker, www.easyriders.com/biker

Street Chopper, www.streetchopperweb.com

American Rider, www.americanrider.com

Motorcycle Cruiser, www.motorcyclecruiser.com

Hot Bike, www.hotbikeweb.com

American Motorcyclist, www.amadirectlink.com

In The Wind, www.easyriders.com/inthewind

IronWorks, www.ironworksmag.com

Motorcyclist, www.motorcyclistonline.com

RoadBike, www.roadbikemag.com

RoadRUNNER, www.roadrunner.travel

Robb Report Motorcycling, www.motorcyclingmag.com

Super Streetbike, www.superstreetbike.com

The Horse: Backstreet Choppers, www.ironcross.net

Thunder Press, www.thunderpress.net

V-Twin, www.easyriders.com/vtwin

Walneck's Classic Cycle Trader, www.walnecks.com

Motorcycle Consumer News, www.mcnews.com

Aftermarket Parts and Riding Gear

Your local Harley dealer will have all the gear, parts, and accessories to make you look like…well, like a rube with a high credit limit who doesn't know what he's doing. Remember what I said: Get to know your bike for a while before you load it up with useless crap. When you're ready, you can hit the dealership or one of these quality aftermarket companies for the stuff to look and feel good, and ride better. Get on their mailing list and you'll always have catalogs to drool over.

Küryakyn

These guys make great tank and saddle bags, but they also carry a lot of dress-up parts for your sled like chrome foot controls, custom handlebars, lighting, and more. www.kuryakyn.com

Aerostich

Riding suits, jackets, pants, helmets, gloves, tank bags, etc…if you wear it, they have it. It's not black leather and fringe, but there's something here for every style of biker. www.aerostich.com

Dennis Kirk

These guys have a huge selection of Harley products, from the gear and accessories to frames and engines for a full custom build. www.denniskirk.com

J&P Cycles

These guys are like a catch all for biker parts and gear. They carry just about everything from just about every manufacturer. Their catalog is like a phone book, but infinitely more entertaining. www.jpcycles.com

JC Whitney

This is a good site for the occasional bargain hunter. Good selection and a lot of quality parts and surprisingly low prices. www.jcwhitney.com

National Cycle

These guys make amazing windshield and fairing accessories, but they also carry saddlebags, aftermarket fenders, and other quality parts for the guys who prefer the bugs and wind. www.nationalcycle.com

Harley-Davidson

The original source for official parts and riding gear. Check it out if you don't have a dealer close to you, or if you just want to browse the selection in your underpants. www.harley-davidson.com

Custom Chrome

This is one of the largest and most popular aftermarket companies, and they specialize in Harley stuff. Most custom builders have a steady account with these guys. Their extensive catalog is available in print or online. www.customchrome.com

JIMS USA

Besides having a ton of parts, engines, and accessories, they also carry all the special Harley-specific tools. If you plan on working on your bike (and every biker should), you'll want to bookmark their website. www.jimsusa.com

Paughco

These guys specialize in obscure and cool parts and accessories for custom builders. Good prices on quality parts. And they have everything from nuts and bolts to frames and tanks. www.paughco.com

INDEX

1%ers, 15, 17

A1A, 67, 72, 103, 105, 106, 124

Aladdin, Wyoming, 149–151

American Chopper, 14

American Iron Horse, 22, 54

American Iron Magazine, 6

American Thunder, 6, 9–11, 86, 98, 150, 152, 155, 157, 163

AMF (American Machine and Foundry), 18, 109

Arlen Ness: The King of Choppers, 55

Arnette, 39

Badlands, 76, 77, 128–132

Bag Tech, 87

Barbieri, Edmund, 7, 10, 19, 20, 23, 25, 34

Barger, Sonny, 36

Bear Mountain, 23

Big Dog Motorcycles, 22, 54

Bikers for Jesus, 36

Biketoberfest, 163

Blue Knights, 23

Bourget, 54

Bragg, Jerry and Colleen, 164

Broken Spoke Saloon, 93

Buell, Eric, 27

Buffalo Chip Campground, 157

Carlisle Bike Fest, 9

Carolina, 37, 41

Chica's Custom Cycles, 59

Chippewa, 37, 41

Chuck Taylor, 88

Colorado River, 162

Cox, Paul, 58

Crazy Horse, 128

Custer State Park, 76, 77, 127, 144

Custom Chrome Inc., 44

Daddy-O, 58

Daily Direct, 85

Daytona Beach International Airport, 114

Daytona Bike Week, 9, 17, 18, 25, 42, 52, 63, 67, 70–72, 74, 75, 80, 83, 85, 87, 97, 99–125, 156, 161, 163

Deadwood, 76, 77

Desmedt, Larry. *See* Indian Larry

Devils Tower, 76, 77, 127, 149–151

Dickies, 35, 89

Discovery Channel, 13, 14, 17, 57

DOT (Department of Transportation), 34, 35, 103

Drag Specialties, 44

Easy Rider, 14, 17

Easyriders magazine, 6

Excelsior, 22

Exile Cycles, 60

Exotic Cycles, 43

EZ-load, 83

Fonda, Peter, 14, 35

FOX, 54

Fremont Street, 162

Frye, 37, 41

Full Throttle Saloon, 69, 155–159, 163

Gasoline Alley, 58

Glenco, 69, 70

Granada Bridge, 123

Hard Way, 56

Harley-Davidson, 10, 11, 14, 15, 17–20, 22, 23, 25, 27–32, 35, 40, 43, 45–47, 50–52, 61, 78, 86, 87, 106, 109, 112, 114, 123, 144, 152

    Buell, 27, 28, 40

    Destroyer, 27

    Dyna Glide, 30

    Evolution, 142

    Fatboy, 65, 106, 111–114

    Heritage, 31, 32, 43, 80, 108–111

    Night Train, 52

    Road Glide, 87

    Screamin' Eagle, 27

    Shovelhead, 142, 143

    Softail, 30, 31, 45–47

    Sportster, 27, 28, 30, 77, 78, 40

    Springer Bad Boy, 48, 51–53, 67, 98

    Ultra Glide, 152

    Ulysses, 27

    V-Rod, 27, 28, 40

    XLCH Sportster, 19–21

Hell's Angels (movie), 17

Hell's Angels, 17, 36, 93, 94

HOG (Harley Owners Group), 35, 36, 41, 93

Hollister, California, 15

Holly Hill, Florida, 118–120, 154

Hollywood Reporter, The, 10

Honda, 17, 23, 25

  350, 23, 25, 66

  Shadow, 19

Hughes, Howard, 17

Indian Larry Legacy, 58

Indian Larry, 58, 59

Indian, 19

Interior, South Dakota, 132, 134

International Supershow, 9

Iron Horse Saloon, 63, 120, 122, 123

J&P Cycles, 44, 109

James, Jesse, 11, 13, 57

Joe Millionaire, 54

John Anderson Drive, 123

Kali Kruiser, 57

Kawasaki, 23, 25, 34

Kid Rock, 155–158

Koezj, John, 7, 10

Küryakyn, 44, 49, 78, 87, 89, 108

Laconia Bike Week, 37, 53, 67, 72, 97–99, 161

Las Vegas Bike Week, 162

Last Resort, 18

Laughlin River Run, 9, 162

Levi's, 35

Lichter, Michael, 55

Lollipops, 106, 124

Mad Max, 60, 103

Maida, Chris, 6

Miller's, 109, 110

Mitchell, Russell, 60

Molly Brown's, 106

Motorcycle Mania, 13, 14, 17, 57

Mount Rushmore, 76, 77, 127

Needles Highway, 142–144

Ness Enterprises, 55

Ness, Arlen, 22, 54, 55, 148, 149

Nichols, Dave, 6

Oakley, 39

Ocean Deck, 125

Old Mission Scooters, 11, 99

Ormond Beach, 123
Other Place, The, 67
Outlaw Bikers From Hell, 17
Packard, 134–136, 138, 139
Panhead, 10, 43
Performance Machine, 44, 56
Phantom, 46, 49, 88
Pink Pony, The, 106, 108, 118, 124
Pissed Off Bastards, 17
Pope, 22
Rapid City Harley-Davidson, 86, 87
Rat's Hole show, 103
Roland Sands Design, 56
Rolling Stones, 17
Rooke Customs, 57
Rooke, Jesse, 57
Rossmeyer, Bruce, 123
ROT Rally, 163, 164
Rumbler, 59
Sampson, 45
Sands, Roland, Nancy, and Perry, 56
Sankyo Company, 17
Schwinn, 57
Seeger, Elisa and Bobby Jr., 58
Shark Lounge, The, 106
Smith, Michele, 8, 9
SmoothNess, 55, 148, 149
Spearfish, South Dakota, 147
SPEED Channel, 6, 9
Sturgis Bike Week, 9, 17, 57, 63, 64, 67, 69, 71, 72,
    75–78, 86, 92, 93, 97, 99, 125–159, 161, 164
Supertrapp, 45
T-Bag, 78, 87, 116
Thunder Mountain Custom Cycles, 54
Triumph, 7
Vance & Hines, 45
Vasko, Johnny, 64
Victory, 22
Villanueva, John, 10, 11, 99, 100
Von Zipper, 39
V-Twin magazine, 6
Wall, Bill, 40
Wild One, The, 17
World War II, 14, 15, 17, 43
Yamaha, 23, 25, 152

Here are some titles you might be interested in picking up. They're all about the biker lifestyle or keeping your bike on the road. And they're all from my publisher, Motorbooks, and available on their website: www.motorbooks.com.

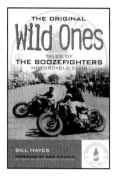

The Original Wild Ones
978-0-7603-2193-5, 139603

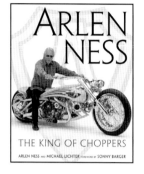

Arlen Ness:
The King of Choppers,
978-0-7603-2219-2, #139395

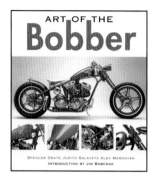

Art of the Bobber
978-0-7603-2531-5, #142993

Dave Perewitz: Chopper Master
and King of Flames,
978-0-7603-2384-4, #140303

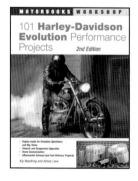

101 Harley-Davidson
Evolution Performance Projects
978-0-7603-2085-3, #139849

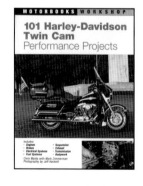

101 Harley-Davidson Twin-Cam
Performance Projects
978-0-7603-1639-9, #136265